Jonathan Weaver

Divine Providence

Jonathan Weaver

Divine Providence

ISBN/EAN: 9783337779856

Printed in Europe, USA, Canada, Australia, Japan

Cover: Foto ©Lupo / pixelio.de

More available books at **www.hansebooks.com**

DIVINE PROVIDENCE

BY

BISHOP JONATHAN WEAVER, D. D.

"The lot is cast into the lap; but the whole disposing thereof is of the Lord."—Prov. 16:33.
"For of him, and through him, and to him, are all things; to whom be glory forever."—Rom. 11:36.

DAYTON, OHIO:
UNITED BRETHREN PUBLISHING HOUSE.
1891.

CONTENTS.

	PAGE.
Introduction	5

CHAPTER I.

| The existence of God | 9 |

CHAPTER II.

| Harmony and perfection of the attributes of God in the government of the world | 30 |

CHAPTER III.

| History of the doctrine of providence—Bible and pagan notions contrasted | 53 |

CHAPTER IV.

| Providence, its nature and reasonableness.—Scripture view of it | 75 |

CHAPTER V.

| Providence, particular and general | 95 |

CHAPTER VI.

| Providence—universal | 120 |

CHAPTER VII.

| Providence overruleth all things. Good and evil are controlled by him | 146 |

CHAPTER VIII.

Providence—mysterious... 70

CHAPTER IX.

Consolation derived from a belief in the doctrine of providence. Omniscience, omnipotence, and omnipresence of God.. 194

CHAPTER X.

Consolation arising from a belief in the doctrine of providence—continued. Immutability, justice, and veracity of God... 218

CHAPTER XI.

Consolation arising from a belief in the doctrine of providence—continued. The goodness, sufficiency, long-suffering, and mercy of God... 244

CHAPTER XII.

Consolation derived from a belief in the doctrine of providence—continued. Love, afflictions, and chastisements..... 269

CHAPTER XIII.

The necessity, importance, and encouragement to submit to the providence of God... 295

INTRODUCTION.

The history of the past as well as the events of the present are exponents of God's providence. "Providence is the light of history, and the soul of the world." A universe without a God and a God without a providence are contradictions. All stand as living witnesses to testify that an all-wise, all-powerful, and benevolent Being is managing the affairs of the universe. Wherever we turn our eye, we see unmistakable evidences of design; and wherever we see such evidences of design, we see proof of the prior existence of the designer. Whence all this harmony, and all this adaptation of one thing to another? Is it all the result of chance? Nay, this can not be, for confusion is the law of chance. The primary signification of the word "providence" is to provide; hence we see in all the arrangements of nature a provision and adaptation as wonderful as they are wise and benevolent. There is a power that pervades and actuates the world of matter and mind. The whole series of events in nature proceeds not by accident, but according to a wise provision made in advance. Accident, chance, and fortune are words often used but seldom understood. In the sense in which they are most commonly used, they are meaningless. What is mostly set down as accident or chance is only the mysterious workings of Providence; we see the effect but not the cause.

INTRODUCTION.

> "These are they
> That strove to pull Jehovah from his throne,
> And in the place of heaven's eternal King,
> Set up the phantom Chance."

The Scriptures affirm that God is the governor of the universe, and a consideration of his character, as revealed in his word, points to him as the only being capable of governing a universe in which mind and matter are so mysteriously connected. He is infinite in wisdom, illimitable in power, and glorious in all his attributes and perfections. The doctrine of providence in its relation to human events merely is of vast importance, but when we consider it in its relation to the future destiny of man, it is worthy of our most serious investigation. The Almighty, who carries forward the affairs of his government according to the counsels of his own will, has been pleased to employ innumerable agencies and instrumentalities by and through which to accomplish his own wise purposes. As the rightful owner of all things, he may employ whatever agencies he chooses. Everything, from the little mote that floats in the sunbeam to the highest order of intelligent beings, is under his control, and may be used in carrying forward his grand designs. Everything has a place to fill, and a work to accomplish.

The plan of this work, while it may not contain much new truth, is so arranged that the most ordinary mind can easily comprehend its main thoughts. The writer has not sought to embellish it with rhetorical elegancies, but has aimed to present truth in the simplest form. He seems to have been convinced that a vast number of Christians are daily losing many of the comforts and consolations of religion from the want of a proper understanding of this doctrine. And to assist in getting before the mind some of the leading features of this doctrine, the author has availed himself of the views and opinions of some of the ablest writers that have given attention to the subject. The reader will find a variety of incidents and illustrations not easily forgotten, which have been employed to assist in bringing out the truth. Above all, the word of God is made the standard of proof and appeal.

Harmony with and submission to the operations of divine Providence will bring to the tired, suffering spirit the most lasting consolations of religion. When Malancthon became overanxious and troubled about himself, and the surrounding circumstances, he drove away his anxious fears by saying, "Let *Philip* cease to rule the world." In proportion as men undertake to rule the world, in that proportion their troubles are increased. It is God's business to rule and ours to trust and submit. No event, however dark and mysterious it may be, can be wrong as long as God reigns.

By a perusal of the following pages the reader will find truths, and words of comfort, that will breathe courage into his soul in the hour of trial. Ministers and laymen will find much that is adapted to their wants, and calculated to make them wiser, stronger, and better Christians. The author,—whom I have known intimately for many years,—considering the many weighty responsibilities pressing upon him during the preparation of this work, by producing a volume meeting so fully a real want, and so full of merit, has shown that he has given this subject much thought, and that its importance has lain with much weight upon his heart. With a rich Christian experience and an intimate knowledge of God's word, as well as his extensive observation of men and things, he was eminently fitted to become the author of this volume.

We bespeak for it a wide circulation, and assure all who read it that it will amply repay them for the cost of purchasing and the labor of perusing its pages.

D. K. FLICKINGER.

CHAPTER I.

THE EXISTENCE OF GOD.

"The Almighty King,
Not always in the splendid scene of pomp
Tremendous, on the surrounding tempest 1.., 3,
Or sweeping whirlwind; nor in the awful peal
Of echoing thunder is he always heard,
Or seen in lightning's livid flames; but oft,
When every turbid element is hushed,
In the still voice of nature stands confest
The Lord Omnipotent."

A heathen philosopher being asked what God was, requested a day to consider the question. At the expiration of that day he desired a second, and then a third. When asked why he wished so much time, he replied that the longer he thought of the question the more obscure and difficult it became. The nature of God is above our comprehension. No finite mind, however exalted, can comprehend an infinite mind, such as the Creator of all things must possess. We are required to believe that he is, but not to comprehend what he is. We can know something about his nature and perfections by carefully studying his works as developed in the material universe.

The idea of the existence of one supreme deity has never been entirely lost. Although the majority of the pagan philosophers, as well as the vulgar heathen, were pantheists, and deified almost everything, material and immaterial, yet above all the gods they recognized the being of an "unknown God." It is exceedingly difficult to understand the notions of the heathen in respect to their gods. They had so many superior and inferior deities, that it is almost if not altogether impossible to reckon them up in order. It is said that in modern oriental paganism there are many millions of gods. Varro reckons up no less than thirty thousand within a small extent, and the number continually increasing.

In the "Encyclopedia of Religious Knowledge" we have a summary of the heathen gods reduced to their several classes, in the following order: (1.) Created spirits, angels or demons. (2.) Heavenly bodies, as the sun, moon, and planets, fixed stars, and constellations. (3.) Elements, as air, earth, and ocean. (4.) Meteors. (5.) Minerals: gold, silver, iron, and stone. (6.) Plants: leeks, onions, wheat, and corn. (7.) Fish and serpents. (8.) Insects, such as flies and ants. (9.) Among birds, such as the stork, raven, sparrow-hawk, eagle, ibis, and lapwing. (10.) Fourfooted beasts: the bull-dog, cat, wolf, lion, baboon, etc. (11.) It was also common to place men among their deities. (12.) They adored whatever related to man, as labor, rest, sleep, youth, age, death, virtues, vices, occasion, time, place, infancy, health, fever, fear, love, pain, indignation, shame, opinion, renown, liberty, money, war, peace, and victory. Jupiter was the god of heaven; Neptune, the god of the sea; Mars, the god of war; Apollo, the god of eloquence; Mercury, the god of thieves; Bacchus, the god of wine; and Cupid, the god of love.

Who that lives under the light and influence of the gospel of Jesus Christ is so blinded and bewildered by the power of sin that he can not realize, to some extent at least, the beneficial effects of that system which brings before the mind one supreme, all-wise, just, and merciful God? How sublime that faith which rises far above all created things, and centers in the one First Cause of all,—One who is infinite in wisdom, great in goodness, and transcendently glorious in all his perfections, the Creator and Supporter of the universe. Contrast this with the notions of the heathen, who wandered in the mazes of superstition and darkness, worshiping as many gods as there were worshipers, and often adoring objects inferior to themselves. The belief in the being of a God, such as is revealed in the Bible, is the sunshine and glory of human existence.

The doctrine of the divine existence may be successfully argued from the fact that all nations, from the remotest antiquity, believed in the being of a supreme power. All did not, and do not now, agree as to the nature and character of God, but all agree that there is such a being. Men are so constituted that they can not divorce this conviction from their minds. No doubt many would love to disbelieve it, but they can not escape from their own consciousness. If they close their eyes to all external evidences, there still remains in them the conscious conviction that there is a God. Men will worship something, no matter what that something is, and this is true of all the nations on the face of the earth. Hence, with considerable propriety, man has been styled "a religious animal." The foundation of all religion, whether true or false, is his belief in the existence of some being superior to himself. From whence comes this intuitive conviction? The heathen often worship objects inferior to themselves, such as beasts, birds, serpents, and inanimate substances; but these are only representatives, to their minds, of something above and beyond them. They invariably associate with the objects of their worship the idea of some invisible god.

The existence of God may be inferred from the works in creation. "The painter's soul is thrown into his painting, and the sculptor's and architect's into their statues and buildings; but their souls meanwhile exist apart, and are capable of other acts besides these. In a sense, as true as it is grand, the soul of the Creator is streaming through the order and life of creation; but meanwhile he exists independent of and far above them." Wherever we turn our eyes we may see evident marks of design, which could not and would not be, unless there was first and above all a designer. There is on the table before me a beautiful book. It is handsomely covered, with gilt edges, and gilt letters on the back. I open it and find on the first page a title with a name. I turn over leaves, and find it full of characters called letters. I examine more closely and find the letters grouped together into words, and the words again into sentences, and these again into paragraphs. And thus the book is made up. What now is the most reasonable conclusion? Did this book originate itself, or was it originated and arranged by some designing mind? We say man did it; and so we reason on every piece of mechanism. We find in the works of nature more abundant evidences of design than we can find in any work of art. There is a complete adaptation of one thing to another, not only in one department of nature but in all, which is evidence conclusive that the whole plan of the universe was laid and executed by some wise, designing mind. The eye and the light are suited to each other. Now, if the eye were differently constructed the light, in coming in contact with it, would not produce vision, unless its constitution were also changed. But for the undulating quality of the atmosphere, the pleasures of sound and the charms of music could never be enjoyed. Or if the ear were differently constructed, all the happiness man gathers from this source would be lost, unless there were a corresponding change in the atmosphere also. We sympathize with the deaf; but if this sense had not been arranged in the manner it is, all would be in a like sad condition. "Consider for a single moment the wisdom which is displayed in the harmonious adjustment of the organs of sense to the scenes of external nature. All the scenes of beauty, grandeur, and benignity which surround us, in the earth and heavens, would remain as one mighty blank, unproductive of enjoyment, unless our bodies were thus 'fearfully and wonderfully made.' Ten thousands of vessels, tubes, lenses, muscles, ligaments, membranes, motions, contrivances, and adaptations, beyond the reach of human understanding fully to investigate or to comprehend, must be arranged and act in harmonious concert, before any one sense belonging to man can perceive and enjoy its objects." And yet we are told that all this contrivance and adaptation of one thing to another came into being without any intelligent first cause—that all is the result of chance. There is in nature enough to supply the multiplied wants of all creatures, in all places, all ages, and upon all occasions, and yet no design, and hence no designer.

If we assume that matter is eternal, then we must in some way account for the production of life, and the constant changes of form. If matter at any time produced life and reason, that same property is in matter still, and the same effects must continue forever. There is in man a power which we call reason; but reason is not a property of matter, else it were a property of all matter. Reason is above matter. Now if matter created or produced reason, then it created or produced something greater than itself, and that which is greatest must be God. But reason is not God. If it were, every man would be his own God; and wherever matter exists without reason, it exists without a God. The notion of spontaneous generation I conceive to be utterly opposed to all philosophical uniformitarianism. Life proceeds from life, and from nothing but life. If dead matter, under the influence of pressure, moisture, temperature, gaseous atmosphere, etc., can produce life, these same elements and forces remain, and like results would continue. But evidence has not yet been discovered that life is produced in any such way. It proceeds from life, and not from dead matter.

Arrasmith sums up the evidences of the existence of God in the following order: "The world is a school wherein reasonable souls are taught the knowledge of God. In a musical instrument, when we observe divers strings meet in harmony, we conclude that some skillful musician tuned them. When we see thousands of men in a field, marshaled under several colors, all yielding exact obedience, we infer that there must be a general whose commands they all are subject to. In a watch, when we take notice of great and small wheels, so fitted as to produce an orderly motion, we acknowledge the skill of an artificer. When we come into a printing house, and see a great number of different letters so ordered as to make a book, the consideration hereof maketh it evident that there is a composer, by whose art they were brought into such a form. When we behold a fair building, we conclude it had an architect; a stately ship well rigged and safely conducted to the port, that it hath a pilot. So here. The visible world is such an instrument, army, watch, book, building, ship, as undeniably argueth a God, who was and is the tuner, general, artificer, composer, architect, and pilot of it."

> "Confusion heard His voice, and wild uproar
> Stood ruled, stood vast infinitude confined;
> Till, at His second bidding, darkness fled,
> Light shone, and order from disorder sprung;
> Swift to their several quarters hasted then
> The cumbrous elements, earth, flood, air, fire;
> And this ethereal quintessence of heaven
> Flew upward, spirited with various forms,
> That rolled orbicular and turned to stars
> Numberless, as thou seest, and how they move:
> Each had his place appointed, each his course."

An Arab was asked the question, "How do you know there is a God?" "How do I know," he asked, "whether a camel or a man passed my tent last night? I know by the foot-prints." God's own foot-prints are the very clearest evidences of his existence. The power, wisdom, and benevolence of the Creator are beautifully manifest in every part of nature. It may be seen in the light, heat, rain, snow, vegetation; in the changes of seasons, summer and winter. In the vast field of nature we see in all the arrangements a most wonderful adaptation of one thing to another. When we see any work of art that is curious and complicated, we say at once that some ingenious mind formed it. We do not suppose for a moment that it originated itself, or came into being without an intelligent agent. Yet strange to say, some men have lived who pretended to believe that the whole material universe, with all its complications and adaptations, came into being without any intelligent agency; that the sun, moon, and stars came whirling into existence, took their places, and keep their courses without any known cause; that the leaf, the spire of grass, and the beautiful flower with all its tints and hues, are what they are without an artificer; that summer and winter, spring and autumn, seed-time and harvest, day and night, the propagation of plants, the diversification of animals and vegetables, all came without a God.

Who that has carefully considered the structure of the eye can doubt for a moment the existence of a wise, merciful, and benevolent Creator. Sturmius held that "the examination of the eye was a cure for atheism." Observe that "before the eye could behold a landscape, and be charmed with its beauties, it was requisite that three humors should be formed, of different sizes different densities, and different refractive powers, three coats, or delicate membranes, with some parts opaque and some transparent, some black and some white, some of them formed of *radial* and some with *circular* fiber, composed of threads finer than those of a spider's web. The crystalline humor required to be composed of two thousand very thin spherical laminæ, or scales, lying one upon another, every one of these made up of one single fiber, or finest thread, wound in a most stupendous manner, this way and that way, so as to run several courses and to meet in as many centers." Now all this curious and complicated organization is compressed into a ball, not more than half an inch in diameter. There must also be a variety of muscles, to move this curiously constructed ball upward and downward, to the right and left. Then it must be connected with the brain by what is called the optic nerve. Add to this a numerous assemblage of minute veins, arteries, nerves, lymphatics, glands. Then add the curtain or lid to secure it from danger, and you have some idea of this curious piece of animal machinery. Now, if atheism is true all this came without any intelligent agent or cause,—the mere caprice of chance.

The heavens, by their vastness, beauty, and order, declare the power, wisdom, and glory of the Creator. Look up on any clear night, and behold the unchanging order and beauty of the starry host. See there that same sentinel star guarding the throne of the eternal North. Clouds and storms may intervene for a while to obscure him from our view, but when these are passed away we always know where to look for his watchful eye. Orion is still girt with his bands as of old; not one of them has ever been displaced. Arcturus and his sons travel their eternal rounds; while the sweet influences of Pleiades are still unbound. Rapid and vast changes are going on among men. Kingdoms, empires, and republics rise and fall; generation after generation enters upon the stage of action and then passes away, but the heavenly host in silent grandeur marches on. "There is no madness so extreme, no blindness so dark and debasing, as that of the man who will not see the witness of God in his wonderful works." . One evening when Bonaparte was on his voyage from Egypt, some of his officers were conversing on the existence of God. A number of the company were atheists. It was a clear and beautiful evening. Napoleon was walking to and fro upon the deck of the vessel, apparently absorbed in his own thoughts. Stopping suddenly before them, he said: "Gentlemen, your arguments are very fine; but who made all those worlds beaming so gloriously above us? Can you tell me that?" Not one could answer. There they were as they now are. Who made them? They must have had an origin.

There is so much wisdom, benevolence, and apparent design in the works of creation that it would seem utterly impossible for any one to suppose that they had not an intelligent author. Everything seems to have been calculated with the utmost exactness. Let us consider a few examples. If the air "were a few miles less in hight than it is, men would soon be suffocated; if it were a few miles more, it would be unendurably hot wherever the sun's rays penetrated. Take land and water for another example. If the land were harder than it is, it could not be cultivated; if softer, nothing could be made firm on the surface. If the water of the sea were heavier, the fishes would rise to the surface, and could not swim; if it were lighter, the fish would sink to the bottom and die. Another example is the proportionate size and weight of man and the globe. If a man were conveyed to the moon, he would weigh five times less than on the earth. He might bound up like a grasshopper, and would be easily upset. If the earth were as large as Jupiter, and otherwise as now, our weight would be increased eleven times, and none of us could walk or stand upright." Is all this nice adaptation of one thing to another the result of mere accident? Does it bear the indications of chance? Does it not argue the pre-existence of a designing mind?

"In all the immense, the strange, and old,
Thy presence careless men behold;

> In all the little, weak, and mean,
> By faith be thou as clearly seen.
> Thou teachest not a leaf can grow,
> Till life from thee within it flow;
> That not a speck of dust can be,
> O Fount of Being, save by thee!"

If we turn our attention to the past, it is utterly impossible to conceive of a time when nothing existed; and if it were even possible to grope our way back through an untold number of ages to a time when there was nothing, the difficulty would only be increased, for then we must show how nothing produced something. If it be said that the material universe was produced by the combined action of certain laws, the difficulty is not in the least diminished, for these laws are something, and must have had an origin. And which is the easier, to conceive that all material things suddenly sprang into being without law, or to conceive that nothing produced the laws by which something was made? or are both suppositions alike absurd? If we can conceive of an effect without a cause, or that the effect existed before the cause, then we may be able to tell how the universe came from nothing.

> "There is no God, the fool in secret said;
> There is no God that rules o'er earth or sky.
> Tear off the band that binds the wretch's head,
> That God may burst upon his faithless eye!
> Is there no God? The stars in myriads spread,

If he look up, the blasphemy deny;
While his own features, in the mirror read,
　Reflect the image of divinity.
Is there no God? The stream that silver flows,
　The air he breathes, the ground he treads, the trees,
The flowers, the grass, the sands, each wind that blows,
　All speak of God, throughout one voice agrees,
And, eloquent, his dread existence shows;
　Blind to thyself, ah, see him. fool, in these!"

How much more reasonable is the belief of the Christian as set forth in the formulas of the divine Scriptures. "In the beginning God created the heavens and the earth." "All things were made by him and for him, and without him was not anything made that was made." His faith is that this supreme First Cause was before all things, self-existent, eternal, immutable, omnipotent, omniscient, just, holy, merciful, and righteous altogether; that this infinitely great and glorious God created all things; that the heavens declare his glory and the earth showeth his handiwork. With this belief firmly fixed in the heart, the Christian looks up and over this vast cathedral and sees the work of his Father. The voiceless lips of the flowers become living teachers, and every leaf a book. In the cultivated fields, in the thick woods, in the shady nook, in every star that decks the vaulted heavens, in the silvery streamlet, in the ocean waves, he sees the finger of God.

> "Not a flower
> But shows some touch in freckle, streak, or stain,
> Of his unrivaled pencil. He inspires
> Their balmy odors, and imparts their hues,
> And bathes their eyes with nectar, and includes
> In grains as countless as the sea-side sands,
> The forms with which he sprinkles all the earth."

How cold and cheerless is that philosophy—if it is worthy the name of philosophy—that would banish the Creator from his own creation; that would take him from the throne of the universe, and leave all things in heaven, in earth, and under the earth, without a ruler. Remove from the universe the great Cause and Parent of all, and all created beings are orphans indeed. The past, present, and future are all wrapped in impenetrable mystery. None can tell whence he came nor whither he goeth. We know that we exist, but we know nothing about the source of our being. We know that we are rational, intelligent creatures, and feel that we are accountable somewhere, and to some one besides ourselves, but we know not where or to whom we shall answer. We are mysteriously compounded of matter and mind. The body consists of millions of parts, all so wisely and nicely arranged that each part is designed to minister comfort to some other part. Our organization is a wonderfully complex piece of machinery. Wisdom and skill of the highest order are displayed in our physical and mental constitution. And yet, if atheism is true we have all the evidences of wisdom, power, and design, without an intelligent designer—without any adequate intelligent cause. All came simply from nothing. Man is nothing more than a heap of organized dust, a stalking machine, a speaking head without a soul, a being without responsibility, and without any known destiny beyond the brief space of this present life.

If we contemplate the magnitude and motions of the heavenly bodies, we are overwhelmed with wonder at the greatness of their size and the rapidity of their movements. Myriads of globes and systems are in constant and rapid motion. Planets revolve around suns, planets around planets, at the rate of many thousands of miles every hour. The earth moves at the rate of sixty-nine thousand miles an hour. The star 61 Cygni moves at the astonishing rate of one hundred and seventy-seven thousand miles an hour. Cassiopeia moves three millions of miles a day, or two thousand, one hundred and sixty miles every minute. Venus moves at the rate of eighty thousand miles every hour, or one thousand, three hundred and thirty miles a minute. Mars moves at the rate of fifty-four thousand six hundred miles every hour. Contemplate millions of stars and planets and systems moving in harmony through the measureless depths of space, many of them with a rapidity that baffles all efforts at conception, and can it be that all this grand machinery has been set in motion without the creating and directing of an all-wise and all-powerful God? A heathen philosopher once asked a Christian, "Where is God?" The Christian answered, "Let me first ask you, where is he not?" This God, whose works are so vast and marvelous, is everywhere present to uphold what he has formed. He guides the orbs of heaven with his finger. "The moon revolves around our earth; the earth, with its associate planets, revolves around the sun. The sun, with all its circling planets, moons, asteroids, comets, is rushing along upon a still mightier orbit, thirty-three millions of miles in a year, in a revolution which it will take eighteen hundred thousand years to accomplish. All the infinite host of heaven is grouped into clusters and systems, that revolve orbit within orbit and world around world, until a firmament of millions of suns is balanced by another as great, and all go sweeping together around some mightier center; and so suns, whose light has been millions of years in reaching us, are all rushing, as if driven by hurricanes of infinite power, round some mysterious center still mightier, still more remote." And yet with all this rapid motion there is in this inconceivably vast and complicated system the most perfect order and harmony. Now, if atheism be true all this grand superstructure, whose boundaries stretch to an almost limitless extent into the infinitudes of space, declares that there is no God— that all is the result simply of chance.

But turning from these cold conjectures to the word of God, we have furnished us a most reasonable account of the works of creation. And whilst it is true that we can not comprehend the greatness of that wisdom that planned so vast and glorious a universe, we can see and feel that it is not the result of accident. "We speak," says Mr. John Bates, "of the power of light, heat, water, wind, electricity, beauty, knowledge, holiness, law, life, and death; but none of these, isolated or even in combination, as they operate throughout the universe, can give an adequate idea of the power of Him from whom they came, and whose purposes they serve. We speak of the power of man in his science, mechanism, laws, armies, steamships, etc.; of the power of angels in all the ways revealed in Scripture; but these powers united with the former fall infinitely short of the power of God. The concentrated power of the whole universe, weighed with His, would be lighter than vanity."

This mighty God made the earth by his power, and established the world by his wisdom, and stretched out the heavens by his discretion. He has created systems in such vast profusion that no man can number them, and at the same time holds them every moment under his immediate direction and superintendence. The wisdom, power, and benevolence of the Creator is displayed in every arrangement throughout his immense provinces. He called into existence every ray of light, and gave life to the smallest insects and creatures, so diminutive that millions of them can exist in a single drop of water. And yet with these manifestations of power and wisdom the Christian may with humble confidence look up and say, "Our Father which art in heaven."

But it was not our purpose to dwell at any considerable length upon the subject of the existence of the Divine Being, only so far as it might seem necessary to fix the attention upon this foundation truth. The idea of the divine existence is the basis upon which we rest all our notions of providence. If there is no God, there is no providence. A God without a providence and a providence without a God are self-contradictions. The Creator of all things must be the provider for all things. The same wisdom, power, and benevolence that was displayed in creating all things is necessary to sustain all things. Hence a God and a providence.

"Order is heaven's first law, and this confest,.
Some are, and must be, greater than the rest,
More rich, more wise; but who infers from hence
That such are happier, shocks all common sense."

CHAPTER II.

HARMONY AND PERFECTION OF THE ATTRIBUTES OF GOD IN THE GOVERNMENT OF THE WORLD.

The science called theology includes a knowledge of God, his moral character, nature, works, word, and attributes. The attributes of God, which will form the subject of this chapter, have been distinguished into affirmative and negative, absolute and relative. The majority of writers, however, distinguish them into the communicable and incommunicable attributes. "The incommunicable attributes of God are such as there is no appearance or shadow of in creatures, as independence, immutability, and eternity. Communicable ones are such as are common to God, and of which there is some resemblance in men, as goodness, holiness, wisdom, and justice." A later distinction, and one perhaps equally comprehensive, divides them into natural and moral.

It is not my purpose to enter into a critical discussion of the attributes of God, only so far as it may be necessary to demonstrate the fact that he governs and controls all things in the exercise of his attributes, and that there must be the most absolute harmony in the exercise of all these perfections. God can not perform a single act, either physically or morally, by the exercise of any one of his attributes that would in the least degree conflict with any other perfection of his nature. An argument based upon the power, wisdom, goodness, and benevolence of God is not complete unless it can be shown that it is in perfect harmony with the justice of God. Proper views of this subject will assist in understanding many things that must otherwise remain obscure. Thus also we have the only safe method of interpreting the operations of divine providence. Whatever God does, however mysterious it may be to us at the time, is wise, benevolent, and just.

IMMUTABILITY. The immutability of God implies that he is unchangeable; that he was, is, and ever will be the same. He is unchangeable in his essence. "Every good gift and every perfect gift is from above, and cometh down from the Father of lights, with whom is no variableness, neither shadow of turning." James i. 17. "But thou art the same, and thy years shall have no end." Ps. cii. 27. He is immutable in his promises. "For I am the Lord, I change not; therefore ye sons of Jacob are not consumed." Mal. iii. 6. He is immutable in his threatenings. "Then shall he say also unto them on the left hand, Depart from me, ye cursed, into everlasting fire, prepared for the devil and his angels." Matt. xxv. 41. God is immutable in his love and mercy. "His mercy endureth forever."

The immutability of God, in his promises and threatenings, is not to be disproved, simply because the evil threatened and the good promised are not always accomplished. God's promises and threatenings are always conditional, either expressed or implied. When he threatens or promises to do this or that, and it is not done, the change is always in man. God threatens to punish the wicked with everlasting destruction; but if the wicked man will forsake his evil way and turn to the Lord, he will be saved. God's threatenings and promises relate to *character*, rather than to men abstractly considered. "At what instant I shall speak concerning a nation, and concerning a kingdom, to pluck it up, and to pull down, and to destroy it; if that nation, against whom I have pronounced, turn from their evil, I will repent of the evil that I thought to do unto them. And at what instant I shall speak concerning a nation, and concerning a kingdom, to build and to plant it; if it do evil in my sight, that it obey not my voice, then I will repent of the good, wherewith I said I would benefit them."

Jer. xviii. 7-10. In these scriptures are presented the *decrees of God;* but all are conditional. That he will punish the wicked, if they continue, is a decree that is unalterably fixed; but if they will turn from their wickedness, he will as certainly pardon them. It is unalterably fixed that God will give or withhold the blessings of salvation, according to the conditions expressed in the verses quoted. Nor does this in the least degree affect the immutability of God. He is ever the same, and his years never change.

ETERNITY OF GOD. This attribute expresses continuance of being; that God is without beginning, end, or succession. That he is without beginning, says Dr. Gill, may be proved from: First. His necessary self-existence. "And God said unto Moses, I AM THAT I AM: and he said, Thus shalt thou say unto the children of Israel, I AM hath sent me unto you." Ex. iii. 14. Second. From his attributes, several of which are declared to be eternal. "For the invisible things of him from the creation of the world are clearly seen, being understood by the things that are made, even his eternal power and Godhead; so that they are without excuse." Rom. i. 20. Third. The eternity of God may be proved from the covenant of grace. "Although my house be not so with God; yet he hath made with me an everlasting covenant, ordered in all things, and sure." II. Sam. xxiii. 5. "But thou, Beth-lehem Ephratah, though thou be little among the thousands of Judah, yet out of thee shall he come forth unto me that is to be ruler in Israel; whose goings forth have been from of old, from everlasting." Mic. v. 2. That he is without end may be proved from: First. His spirituality and simplicity. "And changed the glory of the incorruptible God into an image made like unto corruptible man." Rom. i. 23. Second. From his independency. Rom. vi. 5. Third. From his immutability. II. Pet. i. 24. Fourth. From his dominion and government, said never to end. Jer. x. 10; Dan. iv. 3.

For the benefit of such as may desire to pursue this particular thought farther, I will add a few passages of scripture bearing directly upon the eternity of God: "The eternal God is thy refuge, and underneath are the everlasting arms." Deut. xxxiii. 27. "Before the mountains were brought forth, or ever thou hadst formed the earth and the world, even from everlasting to everlasting, thou art God." Ps. xc. 2. "Who hath wrought and done it, calling the generations from the beginning? I the Lord, the first, and with the last; I am he." Is. xli. 4. "Hearken unto me, O Jacob and Israel, my called; I am he; I am the first, I also am the last." Is. xlviii. 12. "I am

Alpha and Omega, the beginning and the ending, saith the Lord, which is, and which was, and which is to come, the Almighty." Rev. i. 8. See Job xxxvi. 26; Romans i. 20; Psalms xciii. 2; cii. 12, 24, 26; I. Timothy vi. 15, 16; II. Peter iii. 8.

God is also without succession. He was before all things; the same yesterday, to-day, and forever. His duration can not proceed by days and years; if it did, he could not be immutable, for he would be older one day than he was before. "His knowledge proves him without successive duration, for he knows all things, past, present, and to come; he sees the present without a medium, the past without recollection, and the future without foresight."

> "Ere mountains reared their forms sublime,
> Or heaven or earth in order stood,
> Before the birth of ancient time,
> From everlasting thou art God."

OMNIPOTENCE OF GOD. This implies almighty power. This power may be seen: First. In the creation of the universe. "For the invisible things of him from the creation of the world are clearly seen, being understood by the things that are made, even his eternal power and Godhead." Rom. i. 20. "In the beginning God created the heaven and the earth." Gen. i. 1. "He hath made the earth by his power, he hath established the world by his wisdom, and hath stretched out the heavens by his discretion." Jer. x. 12. Second. The omnipotence of God is exhibited in the preservation of all his creatures. "For by him were all things created, that are in heaven, and that are in earth, visible and invisible, whether they be thrones, or dominions, or principalities, or powers: all things were created by him, and for him: and he is before all things, and by him *all things consist.*" Col. i. 16, 17. "Thou, even thou, art Lord alone; thou hast made heaven, the heaven of heavens, with all their host. the earth, and all things that are therein, the seas, and all that is therein, and *thou preservest them all.*" Neh. ix. 6. Heb. i. 3. Ps. xxxvi. 6. Third. This power was displayed in the stupendous work of human redemption. "And the angel answered and said unto her, The Holy Ghost shall come upon thee, and the *power* of the Highest shall overshadow thee: therefore also that holy thing which shall be born of thee shall be called the Son of God. * * * For with God *nothing* shall be impossible." Luke i. 35, 37. "And what is the exceeding greatness of his *power* to us-ward who believe, according to the working of his *mighty power*, which he wrought in Christ, when he raised him from the dead." Eph. i. 19, 20. Fourth. His power may also be seen in the continuation and success of the gospel in the world. It shall continue to increase. Matt. xiii. 31, 32. It shall be preached to all people. Matt. xxviii. 18–20; Matt. xvi. 14. Fifth. The power of God shall be displayed in the resurrection of the body. I. Cor. xv.

> "The Hand that built the palace of the sky,
> Formed the light wings that decorate a fly;
> The Power that wheels the circling planets round,
> Rears every infant floweret on the ground;
> That Bounty which the mightiest beings share,
> Feeds the least gnat that gilds the evening air."

THE SPIRITUALITY OF GOD. Spirit is that which thinks, and performs all the operations of intelligence, and possesses inherent powers of action, without being acted upon. No man can fully comprehend what spirit is. Matter is known by certain phenomena, such as impenetrability, extension, inertia, and so on; but spirit possesses none of these qualities. A thing may be spiritual without being pure spirit. Paul, when describing the nature of the resurrection body, says it shall be spiritual, that is, it shall partake of the nature of spirit, but it will not be spirit in the sense in which God is a spirit. "The spirituality of God is demonstrable from the contradictions necessarily resulting from the contrary supposition. No two particles of matter can exist in the same place; wherever, therefore, we admit of a material creature, we exclude the possibility of a material deity, if such an expression may be at all allowed." Power, wisdom, and universal presence are not properties of matter, but superior to it. The Bible affirms that "God is a spirit." John iv. 24. "The Lord is that spirit." II. Cor. iii. 17. "The spirit of God moved upon the face of the waters." Gen. 1. 2. To the three persons in the Godhead this one nature is common.

Omnipresence of God. This attribute implies that he is in all places, and fills all space at all times. We can not see him, for he is invisible; neither can we see the mind of man, nor the wind that bloweth where it listeth. If God is not omnipresent, he is not competent to govern the universe, nor is he a proper object of worship. "But will God indeed dwell on the earth? Behold, the heaven and heaven of heavens can not contain thee." I. Kings viii. 27 "Whither shall I go from thy Spirit? or whither shall I flee from thy presence? If I ascend up into heaven, thou art there: if I make my bed in hell, behold, thou art there. If I take the wings of the morning, and dwell in the uttermost parts of the sea; even there shall thy hand lead me, and thy right hand shall hold me." Ps. cxxxix. 7–10. "Do not I fill heaven and earth? saith the Lord." Jer. xxiii. 24; Amos ix. 2, 3.

ATTRIBUTES OF GOD.

God is everywhere. All things are full of, yet distinct from him. "The cloud on the mountain is his covering; the muttering from the chambers of the thunder is his voice; that sound on the top of the mulberry trees is his 'going;' in that wind, which bends the forest or curls the clouds, he is walking." God is everywhere by his power, wisdom, and goodness; ruling, controlling, supporting, and beholding. "Thou, God, seest me." Every one is God-inclosed, God-filled, and God-breathing. The almighty, all-pervading Spirit is everywhere. All those passages wherein the presence of God is promised to the Christian, go to prove his omnipresence. There is not a Christian, however poor and obscure among men, but that may claim his presence at all times and in all places. When poor and forsaken by men, persecuted and tempted, scorned and derided, at home or abroad, among friends or foes, in health or dying, how divinely sweet the reflection steals over the soul, "Thou, God, seest me."

> "In vain on wings of morn we soar,
> In vain the realms of space explore,
> In vain retreat to shades of night,—
> For what can veil us from thy sight?
> Distance dissolves before thy ray,
> And darkness kindles into day."

OMNISCIENCE OF GOD. This implies that he knoweth all things; that his knowledge is infinite, eternal, universal, and perfect. This attribute is peculiar to himself. To suppose, as some divines have done, that God determines not to know certain things is a reflection upon his character. "Talk no more so exceeding proudly; let not arrogancy come out of thy mouth: for the Lord is a God of knowledge, and by him actions are weighed." I. Sam. ii. 3. "Shall any teach God knowledge? seeing he judgeth those that are high." Job xxi. 22. "For he looketh to the ends of the earth, and seeth under the whole heaven." Job xxviii. 24. "O Lord, thou hast searched me, and known me. Thou knowest my downsitting and mine uprising; thou understandest my thoughts afar off. Thou compassest my path and my lying down, and art acquainted with all my ways. For there is not a word in my tongue, but, lo, O Lord, thou knowest it altogether. Thou hast beset me behind and before, and laid thine hand upon me. Such knowledge is too wonderful for me; it is high. I can not attain unto it." Ps. cxxxix. 1–6. "Great is our Lord, and of great power: his understanding is infinite." Ps. cxlvii. 5. "Known unto God are all his works from the beginning of the world. Acts xv. 18. Rom. xi. 33–36.

If these passages teach anything at all, they teach the omniscience of God. "His understanding is infinite." He seeth all things, and knoweth all things. He is a God of knowledge and understanding. The thoughts of the heart are all open before him. All the plans and purposes of men are known to him. A being of less knowledge could not govern a universe. He must know all things, in order to provide for all things.

The Justice of God. "The justice of God is that perfection of the divine nature from which arises the absolute rectitude of his moral government." This attribute is essential to the very being of God. Without it he would be unfit to govern the world, and to judge the whole earth. God is not only just in himself, but just in all his administrations. Two elements in his moral government display this attribute: First. Remunerative justice, by which he distributes rewards to all who comply with the conditions of the gospel. "If ye sow to the Spirit, ye shall of the Spirit reap life everlasting." "To him that overcometh, I will give a crown of life." Second. Punitive justice. He can not and will not let sin go unpunished. If those who sow to the Spirit reap life everlasting, then those who sow to the flesh must reap corruption. "Whatsoever a man soweth, that shall he also reap." That is just.

On the nature of divine justice, Mr. Ambrose gives a striking illustration: "When God appointed a surety, his Son, and charged our debts upon him to satisfy his justice, in that God would not spare his Son in the least degree of punishment; hereby the Lord shows a stronger love to justice than if he had damned ten thousand thousand creatures. Suppose a malefactor comes before a judge, the judge will not spare the malefactor, but commands satisfaction to the law; this shows that the judge loves justice. But if the judge's own son be a delinquent, and it appears before all the country that the judge now doth more honor justice in this than in condemning a thousand others, so when the Lord shall cast many thousands into hell, there to be tormented throughout eternity, it shows that God loves justice; but when his own Son shall take our sins upon him, and he will not spare him, this surely declares God's love to righteousness more than if all the world should be damned."

The justice of God is most abundantly set forth in the Scriptures. "He is the Rock, his work is perfect: for all his ways are judgment: a God of truth and without iniquity, just and right is he." Deut. xxxii. 4. "Justice and judgment are the habitation of thy throne: mercy and truth shall go before thy face." Ps. lxxxix. 14. "There is no God else beside me; a just God and a Savior." Isa. xlv. 21. See also Ps. xix. 8, 9; Ex. xxiii. 7; Prov. xxiv. 12; Rev. xv. 3.

Add to these the sovereignty, goodness, mercy, benevolence, love, holiness, veracity, sufficiency, patience, long-suffering, and vengeance of God, and you have before your mind the character that governs the universe. And as we contemplate the attributes and absolute perfections of the Divine Being, we must see in him every conceivable fitness to govern all things. There is everything to comfort the hearts of all that will trust in him, and enough to alarm all that attempt to withstand him. "If I speak of strength, lo, he is strong: and if of judgment, who shall set me a time to plead?" Job ix. 19. "God hath spoken once; twice have I heard this; that power belongeth unto God." Ps. lxii. 11. "Behold, the nations are as a drop of a bucket, and are counted as the small dust of the balance: behold, he taketh up the isles as a very little thing." Is. xl. 15. "Cry out and shout, thou inhabitant of Zion: for great is the Holy One of Israel in the midst of thee." Is. xii. 6.

The primary idea of government is guidance, direction, and control in accordance with rule. Moral government implies the administration of moral law; it presides over and seeks to control the free will. Physical government "presides over and controls physical states, and changes of substances or constitutions, and all involuntary states and changes." The providential government of God may be considered as that disposal of his creatures, and all events relating to them, in accordance with his wisdom, justice, immutability, and goodness.

God is the only being in the universe, of which we have any knowledge, that is capable of governing the world. He is immutable, hence always the same; eternal, was before all things; omnipotent, has all power; omniscient, knoweth all things; omnipresent, is everywhere at the same time; just, and can not do wrong. He is holy, good, benevolent, merciful, patient, and long-suffering. A being in whom all these attributes and perfections center, is in every way capable of governing both matter and mind. Hence the following conclusions are justly drawn: First. In his moral government, he renders to every intelligent being full and complete justice. Second. In his providential government, he disposes of all his creatures, and all the events with which they may be surrounded, according to his wisdom, justice, power, and goodness. Third. In his spiritual government he maintains, by the agency of his Spirit and the instrumentality of his word, a constant control over the hearts and minds of his people; so that all the affairs in the universe are governed in a manner so as not to interfere with

ATTRIBUTES OF GOD.

his sovereignty, nor the free will of man, and at the same time accomplish for his creatures the highest possible good.

There is in all these attributes of the Godhead the most complete and absolute harmony; and nothing can occur in his physical, moral, providential, or spiritual government that is not in harmony with all the attributes and perfections of his nature. He can not perform a single act, by the exercise of any one of his attributes or perfections, that will either directly or indirectly conflict with any other of his attributes or perfections. To illustrate: God is omnipotent, yet he does not do everything. If this attribute were exercised independently of all the rest, he might either save or destroy the whole race of man, irrespective of moral character. But this would either conflict with his justice or goodness. His goodness, love, benevolence, and mercy might prompt him to save all men. But he is immutable, and can never love more than he loves now. If these perfections of his nature would ever prompt him to save all men irrespective of moral character, they would prompt him to save them at once. If not, then he is not immutable. These attributes and perfections can only be exercised in accordance with the principles of a perfectly righteous, moral government. "God himself is limited by the immutable perfections of his own nature in the modes of operation for the salvation of sinners, and can not depart from the essential conditions upon which he has proposed that fallen man can be made a partaker of the divine nature. The slightest departure therefrom would shake the very pillars of heaven."

Complicated and inexplicable as many of the providences of God may be, yet, when understood, they will be seen to be in perfect harmony with all the attributes and perfections of his character. God is not bound by any obligations to communicate to us what his plans and purposes are. Whatever is essential to our present or eternal salvation he will reveal at the right time. The promise of God is, that in due time the glass through which we now see darkly will be removed, and we shall see as we are seen, and know as we are known. For the present we should learn to be content with the simple faith that the "Judge of all the earth will do right."

In the first chapter of the book of Ezekiel there is presented a most beautiful and grand illustration of the nature of God's government. The reader would do well to turn to the chapter and read it carefully. Whatever else the Almighty intended to teach by this wonderful vision, it serves to illustrate the nature of his providential dealings with men and nations. This vision may very properly be "epitomized as a representation of the march of God in the chariot of his providence, through the successive ages of the world."

The first object in the vision that attracts our attention is the appearance of the living creatures, which "ran and returned as the appearance of a flash of lightning." In this age of rationalism on the one hand and Spiritualism on the other, it is difficult to explain to the satisfaction of either party the plain, unambiguous meaning of any part of God's word. A careful study of the holy Scriptures will, however, warrant us in the belief that God in part carries on the affairs of his government by the ministry of men and angels; for "he maketh his angels spirits, and his ministers a flame of fire." And this subserviency of men and angels in the execution of his plans and purposes, serves to impress our minds with the truth that all are servants of God. Every creature in heaven and in the earth, together with all the elements, is under his control, and may at any time and in any manner be employed to execute his purposes. He may employ an angel or a legion of angels to carry out his plans. He may employ a bird, a fish, an insect, if he chooses, for all are made to serve him, and all stand in attitude of waiting, like the "living creatures," ready to go forward or return at his command. They all go straight forward, as directed by his wisdom, accomplishing results sometimes that reach far into the future. The old world was destroyed by water; the cities of the plain by fire; Baalam was reproved by the ass; the prophet was fed by ravens; Jonah was brought to the shore by a fish; the Egyptians were scourged by flies and frogs. He may employ the wind, famine, pestilence, war, lightning, and tempest to do his bidding. All are his servants, and he may use any one of them or any number of them. He may thrash a mountain with a worm, and send an angel to protect a spire of grass. It is his absolute prerogative to employ such agencies and instrumentalities as his own wisdom may dictate for the accomplishment of his designs.

Next in order we have the vision of the wheels. "Their rings, they were so high that they were dreadful," and, to add to the grandeur of their appearance, "they were full of eyes." These are the wheels of divine providence, and indicate to us the various changes and revolutions which occur in order that the divine purposes of God may be accomplished. Their being full of eyes denotes that all the vast changes and revolutions of time, in all places, and under every conceivable circumstance, are directed, controlled, or overruled by the same unerring hand. "The events of time are all directed by an infinite intelligence; there is an end, a design, in every turn of providence; every movement of the wheel has an object, and to that object do the eyes never cease to turn."

We are now directed to the appearance of a wheel in a wheel. This at once suggests the idea of complication, and of retrograde motion,—one wheel revolving one way and the other in the opposite direction. Nevertheless, the prophet is particular to state, once or twice, that when the living creatures went, the wheels went,—"they all went straight forward." Now the ways of Providence are often intricate and mysterious to us, and sometimes appear to be contradictory. But if we were permitted to see all the designs and purposes of the Almighty, we would at once be convinced that all his ways are wise and just. We see and understand only in part, and hence, in our blindness, we often think his ways are unequal. Why he does this and that we are not at present permitted to know. We see *through a glass darkly*. Jacob, in the anguish of his heart, said, "All these things are against me." Joseph was gone, and now Benjamin was demanded; he must go in sorrow to the grave. He saw the appearance of a wheel in a wheel. To his mind there was not only complication in the movement of the wheels, but actually

4

a retrograde motion, a moving backward instead of forward. He was looking through a glass darkly. But when his sons returned from Egypt and told him that Joseph was still living, and that all the necessary arrangements had been made to take the entire household down to Egypt where there was bread enough and to spare, the old man saw, for the first time, how straight every thing had gone forward in his case. Then he exclaimed, "It is enough, my son Joseph liveth; I will go and see him before I die." Thus it will be in the end; when the plans and purposes of God are understood, all will exclaim, "He hath done all things well."

Another peculiarity about this machine was, that "the wheels were so high that they were dreadful." This indicates that the plans of God are in many respects far above our comprehension, reaching from the beginning to the end. In our present condition we are only permitted to see detached parts of his plans, a link here and there, and are unable to put them together. We see in part and understand in part,—only in broken glimpses. "But when, from some pinnacle of the better land, we take a retrospect of the way in which the Lord has led us, we shall see that every turn, and winding, and crossing, and check, and obstruction, and fall, and sickness, and sorrow, were just as necessary to our everlasting happiness, as that Christ should have died, or that the Bible should have been written."

And as it is with individuals so it is with nations. All the various revolutions and apparent complications in the movement of the machinery have an object, a distinct and definite end; and the wheels will continue to revolve and the machinery move straight forward until all the purposes of God are accomplished. The history of our own country, its struggle for liberty, and its second baptism with blood, are all turnings of the wheels of divine providence. Wisdom, justice, love, and benevolence are in every revolution of the wheels. Some time we may see it in a clearer light than we are able to see it now.

In a subsequent chapter we may dwell more at length upon this particular point. We have introduced it here to assist in illustrating the truth of our proposition, which is, that all the operations of providence, however mysterious and inexplicable they may be, are carried forward in perfect harmony with all the attributes of God. When John saw the saints in heaven "standing as it were upon a sea of glass mingled with fire," they sang this song, "Great and marvelous are thy works, Lord God Almighty; just and true are thy ways, thou King of saints.

DIVINE PROVIDENCE.

"O, all-preparing Providence divine!
   In thy large book what secrets are enrolled,
What sundry helps doth thy great power assign,
   To prop the course which thou intend'st to hold!
What mortal sense is able to define
   Thy mysteries, thy counsels manifold!
It is thy wisdom strangely that extends
Obscure proceedings to apparent ends."

CHAPTER III.

HISTORY OF THE DOCTRINE OF PROVIDENCE—BIBLE AND PAGAN NOTIONS CONTRASTED.

The foundation of all religion, whether true or false, natural or revealed, is the belief in the existence of a God or of a plurality of gods. This proposition is universally conceded. It would be utterly impossible to conceive of any religion at all, if the existence of a superior being were not first admitted. The notion of a Supreme Being was never wholly lost in the pagan world; and while they introduced many strange and superstitious notions into their philosophy, they never denied the existence of God or the gods. They wandered in the mazes of superstition and error. They reasoned well on many things, but were never able to form correct opinions of the true God and his government. Their best notions of the gods were but fragmentary ideas of the true God. Often in attempting to settle the question respecting the gods, their power, wisdom, and justice, "their empirical investigations were abruptly lost in dark uncertainty. Their yearning spirits fluttered against the veil which hides them, and beat it till their wings were weary, and then descended again into the sphere of sense and of cold abstractions from which they had started."

Next to the doctrine of the existence of a Supreme Being is that of an overruling providence. The very notion of a God suggests the idea of a providence. It would be next to impossible to conceive of a God without a providence, or a providence without a God. This the majority of pagan philosophers realized. Cicero, when speaking of those philosophers who taught that the gods take no care of mankind, said: "If their opinions were true there would be no piety, no sanctity, no religion—that if the gods do not mind what men do, or what events befall them, there is no reason to pray to them or worship them; and that if religion and piety be taken away from among men, the greatest confusion and disorder would ensue in human life; and together with piety, mutual fidelity, and the social ties which bind mankind together, and that most excellent virtue justice, would be banished out of the world."

The pagan philosophers, the wisest and best of them, while they held to many strange and superstitious notions respecting the creation and government of the universe, were of the opinion that the gods did exercise some sort of care and concern for the human race—that the events of time were not wholly the results of mere chance. It will doubtless be of interest to the majority of the readers to present in this connection what some of the more considerate philosophers among the heathen have said. It will assist us in comprehending, to some degree at least, the superiority of the Christian doctrine of providence. Men who are wont to boast of the light of nature and the power of human reason; that would exalt it above a divine revelation; that say it were better for the world if the Bible were out of it, are invited to a careful consideration of the subject, by contrasting the opinions and sayings of the wisest and best men that have ever lived without the aid of a divine revelation, with the opinions and teaching of Christian philosophers. We will aim to deal fairly. We can well afford to do so. We will not give the weakest things that have been said by heathen sages, but the purest sentiments that were ever uttered by their greatest and best philosophers.

As far back as we are able to trace the history of men and nations, we shall find that the notion of a providence was held as a part of the universal tradition. It is of course somewhat difficult to follow their traditions, and understand precisely what their opinions were. According to the most reliable authority we have, the majority of the philosophers, as well as the vulgar heathen, were pantheists. And "as they fell from the right knowledge of the one true God, and became more and more immersed in idolatry and polytheism, so their notions of providence became confused and erroneous, and debased with many corrupt mixtures. The providence they acknowledged was the providence of the divinities they adored. It was parceled out among a multiplicity of gods and goddesses, among whom they supposed the administration of all things to be distributed, as being co-rulers with God and sharers with him in his empire."

Plato says, concerning the pagans in his time, that "all those who had never so small a share of sobriety or prudence were wont in the undertaking of any affair, whether small or great, always to invoke God." That is, they invoked the guidance and assistance of some one or all of the gods. It is not necessary, for our present purpose, to point out the gross errors into which they had fallen respecting the character and attributes of the true God. Our chief object is to show that the majority who, in time past, believed in the existence of a God at all, believed also in a providence. Occasionally they uttered some most sublime and beautiful sentiments respecting the gods, as they often did respecting the immortality of the soul, and the future home of the good; but when they would return to their cold abstract reasoning they would contradict everything they had said. When they followed the impulses of their nature they seemed to believe in the existence of God, the immortality of the soul, the future existence of man, and the doctrine of providence. But, "like benighted travelers seeking their way in a dreary wood, rather bewildered than aided by the mimic lights that played around them in the dismal bogs, so "the heathen in their blindness' sought after a better life amid the shadows which hang over the grave. Their light of reason and dim tradition have been so unsteady, and prevailed so feebly against the darkness in which it attempted to shine, that they have often laid down in despair or followed it with a doubting and heavy heart." But wherever they went, and however dreamy and confused their notions were, they carried with them continually

"This secret dread, this inward horror
Of falling into naught."

Socrates said "that the gods know all things both the things which are said and the things which are done, and even the things which are deliberated upon in secret, and that they are everywhere present, and give signification to men concerning all human affairs." But for his polytheism, this passage reads well. He believed in a providence; that all human affairs were directed and controlled by an invisible power, and that this power was held by the gods; but, like the rest of them, he would not have been able to tell to which of the gods any particular event should be ascribed.

There is a passage in the elder Pliny relating to the notions of fortune, as held in his time. "Through the whole world," he says, "in all time, fortune is universally invoked by all persons. This alone has the praise or blame of everything, and is at the same time worshiped and respected; esteemed by the most of mankind to be blind, uncertain, various, and inconstant; a favorer of such as are unworthy. To this all events are attributed, both prosperous and adverse; and in the whole management of human affairs this fills up both sides of the account." Sallust observes that "fortune rules in everything." Menander says, "Fortune is the king or tyrant of all gods." From these extracts it appears that fortune was worshiped as a deity, with whatever attributes or qualities the worshiper had a mind to ascribe to it. It is in evidence farther that among the Greeks and Romans temples were erected and dedicated to this god.

Among the vulgar pagans, the notion very generally prevailed that providence only extended to outward affairs, and hence the gods were applied to for health, riches, and success in temporal matters, but not for wisdom or any of the virtues. Cicero quotes Cato as saying: "All men attribute the external commodities they enjoy, their plenty of corn, wine, oil, and fruits, to the gods; but no man ever acknowledged his having received his virtue from God. For who ever gives thanks to the gods for his being a good man? But for his being possessed of riches and honors, and preserved from dangers, he does. It is on account of these things that they give Jupiter the appellation of *optimus et maximus*, the greatest and the best; not that he makes us just, temperate, and wise, but that he gives us health, safety, and affluence." "This," he adds, "is the judgment of all mankind, that the gifts of fortune are to be asked of God, but that a man is to expect wisdom only from himself." Now while it was the opinion of the learned Cato that the heathen most generally believed that the gods never concerned themselves about anything more than the temporal wants and affairs of mankind, it is evident that some of the philosophers, and even the vulgar among the heathen, had a better way of thinking, as we shall hereafter see.

The Epicureans had a great deal to say against the doctrine of providence as held by the teachers of Christianity. Cæcilius represents it as an absurd thing in the Christian to believe that "their God, whom they can neither see nor show, inspects diligently into the manners of all men, into their actions, and even their words and hidden thoughts; and that he is everywhere present, troublesome, and impertinently busy and curious, since he interesteth himself in all things that are done, and thrusteth himself into all places; whereas he can neither attend to every particular whilst he is employed about the whole, nor be able to take care of the whole, being busied about particulars." This is certainly a cold and chilling speculation, but it is human nature unaided by any divine revelation.

The philosophers who asserted a providence are represented by Epictetus as holding very dissimilar views. "Some of them," he says, "admitted a providence in great and heavenly things, but in nothing upon earth. Others supposed it to take care of things both in heaven and earth, but only in general, not with respect to individuals. Others, like Ulysses in Homer, and Socrates, held that providence extendeth to individuals, and that not the least motion or action can be concealed from God." Plato asserts "that mankind, and the things relating to them, not only in great matters but even the smallest, are under the care of Divine Providence."

The Platonists and many others of the philosophers held to the notion of a universal providence; but this they divided among the deities. He whom they regarded as the chief deity did not concern himself about the affairs of mankind, but committed that to the inferior deities. They did not think that the great God meddled with the things of the world, but rather withdrew himself, with the "supercelestial gods, his companions, from the view of mortals, as being of so sublime a nature that no sharpness of sight or understanding could reach to them." But he brings into view certain celestial deities, such as the sun, moon, and stars. Plutarch argues "that it is unworthy of the majesty of the Supreme Being, and inconsistent with his happiness, to busy himself about the affairs of men." Apuleius, as quoted by Dr. Leland, says "that the supreme God is so far above us, that he is scarcely to be approached by the most purified intellect, and that there is no immediate intercourse between us and the first class of subordinate deities, visible or invisible, but the intercourse is carried on by intermediate powers called demons, who are appointed to take care of everything here below which it is not becoming the majesty of the celestial gods to meddle with."

The deplorable state of darkness, corruption, and superstition into which the heathen mind had fallen, respecting the doctrine of divine providence, grew out of their ignorance of the character of God. It is philosophically true that the worship of the worshiper will be in harmony with his notions of the character he worships. "The names, the character, and the attributes of God were misapplied to a multiplicity of idol deities. Instead of being led by the works of God to acknowledge and adore him, the glorious author, they for the most part worshiped the works themselves, and paid that adoration to them which was due to him alone." And what reason have we to believe that any people under heaven, unaided by a divine revelation from God, would have risen any higher in their notions of the Supreme Being than did the pagan nations? The same sun shone on them that shines on us; the same moon and stars that looked down on them, look down on us; the same laws and forces that operated in nature then, operate in nature now. In a word, the whole course of nature continues about the same. "It would," says Dr. Leland, "argue great arrogance in us to suppose that we have a more comprehensive reach of thought, greater penetration and force of reason, than those sublime geniuses which have been the admiration of all succeeding ages." And yet with all their learning and vast abilities, they were in a measure ignorant of the character of God and his government. "The world by wisdom knew not God."

The Stoics are reckoned as among the more zealous advocates of the doctrine of a divine providence; but, like the majority of those of whom mention has been made, they generally speak of the gods in the plural, and teach "that the world is administered by the providence of the gods." Plutarch, in his tract against Colotes, the Epicurean, says, "There is a providence of the gods, and the sun and moon are animated, whom all men worship, and to whom they offer prayers and sacrifices."

Balbus, who by some writers is regarded as the representative of the Stoic sect, said some excellent things concerning the care which providence exercised over the human race. He taught that men were greatly dependent upon it; that the welfare of individuals or particular persons is consulted, arranged, or provided for by the immortal gods. He did not, however, believe in a universal providence, but that the care and concern of the gods extended to persons of distinction and over great cities. "The gods," he said, "took care of great matters, and neglected small ones." Euripides said that "God only concerns himself with the greatest things, and leaves the smaller to fortune." Cato, from whom we have already quoted, takes great exceptions to the opinions of Balbus and Euripides. He charges them with inconsistency; that if the gods knowingly pass by anything they can not be charged with ignorance, nor the want of power to know and take care of everything; that if the gods do not take care of every individual there could be no good reason to pray to them, "since," he says, "it is by particular persons that prayers and vows are made."

It would not, however, be just to say that all the Stoics believed as Balbus did. Chrysippus taught that Providence extended his care to all things, great and small, and Epictetus and Antonius were of the same opinion. But Seneca did not fully indorse their sentiments. He said that it was proper to know and believe "that the gods presided over the world; that they order things relating to the whole, as what properly belongs to them; and that they exercise a guardianship over the human race, and are sometimes curious about individuals." How cold and cheerless such speculations are, and how little there is in such sentiments to inspire in the human soul a feeling of love and veneration for such a god.

The gods are so little concerned about men, that they may be forgotten, or if not wholly forgotten, they may be left to fight the fierce battles of life alone.

There was a great amount of perplexity and uncertainty among the ancient pagans, both the vulgar and the philosophers, respecting the doctrine of providence. They divided and subdivided the ordering of the concerns of this world between God, fate, and fortune. Some things they ascribed to the gods, some things to fate, and some things to fortune, so that, at this remote period, one can hardly tell what they did believe. Thales said that "necessity is the strongest of all things, for all things are subject to it." Parmenides and Democritus held that "all things came by necessity." Heraclitus believed that "all things are done by fate." According to Plutarch, even Plato referred some things to providence, and some things to necessity. He says that "God, and with God, fortune and opportunity govern all the affairs of men." Maximus Tyrius "supposes that all things which happen to men are either inspected and ordered by providence, or necessitated by fate, or varied by fortune, or managed by human art and skill; that riches, and what are usually called the good things of fortune, are not given by the gods, but are the mad gifts of fortune;

and compares them to the gifts we receive from persons that are drunk."

There must arise in the mind of every reflecting person the conviction of an absolute necessity for something superior to human reason, to guide mankind in matters of such vast moment. The views and opinions of the pagans regarding God, his providence, the immortality of the soul, and a future state of rewards and punishments, were in the main false. We are sometimes almost ready to conclude that the beautiful sentiments which were once in a while uttered by the pagan philosophers and poets respecting their Elysian fields and Hesperian gardens, were nothing more than "philosophical refinements, or perhaps pious frauds on the ignorant." If it were all of life to live here; if man ceased to be when he enters the grave; if there were nothing beyond this world, neither angels nor spirits, then it would not matter so much what men believed. But

> "That mysterious thing,
> Hath no limit from the walls of sense,—
> No chill from hoary time,—with pale decay
> No fellowship,—but shall stand forth unchanged,
> Unscorched amid the resurrection fires,
> To bear its boundless lot of good or ill."

Turning from these cold speculations to the Holy Scriptures, we are taught plainly that the care of the Almighty Creator of all things is extended to all his creatures,—to every individual of the human race, whether he be rich or poor, high or low, learned or unlearned, young or old. And this care extends to all times and includes all places. The scripture sentiment is, that the very hairs of our heads are numbered, and a sparrow can not fall without God's notice. It is a source of the very highest comfort to the Christian to know and feel that the God he serves is everywhere present; that he understands the exact condition of every one; and that although he is so great, that he is incomprehensible to men, yet he condescends to administer to the wants of all his creatures in heaven and in the earth. He is no respecter of persons, and nothing can transpire without his notice. Everything, from the loftiest archangel to the minutest animalcule that sports in a drop of water, is under his sovereign control. He is just and good in all his dispensations. Nothing is left to the guidance of blind chance, or the control of subordinate deities. Omniscient, he understands the conditions and necessities of all his creatures. Omnipresent, he is always near to protect and sustain. Omnipotent, he is able to do all things according to the counsel of his own will.

The pagan philosophers had little to encourage them to trust in their gods, or even to pray to them. Socrates, in his second Alcibiad, represents to that young nobleman that it was not safe to pray for anything in particular. Pythagoras, we are informed, permitted no man to pray for himself. Maximus Tyrius had a whole dissertation to prove that we ought not to pray at all. Some of the philosophers thought differently, but such were their views and opinions of the Divine Being, his character, attributes, and providences. that whatever they might have said on the duty of prayer could have had but little influence over the minds of the masses. They were not sure that the gods took any notice of them in general, and even if they did, they were not at all certain whether that notice would be favorable or otherwise.

Our clearest and best views of a subject are often obtained by the help of contrast. To appreciate the grandeur of a mountain there must also be in near view some wide-spreading plain. To estimate the value of light, we must be thrust into darkness. To understand the value of health, we must be sick. To fix upon the mind and heart something of the superior excellency of the character of the Christian's God, we can not do better, perhaps than to contrast the views held by the pagan philosophers concerning their deities with those expressed by the sacred writers. In the preceding pages of this chapter we have given the very best and purest things that were ever said by the pagans respecting the character of God and the nature of his government. We will now give a view of his character as expressed by the sacred writers.

1. *Compared with other gods.* "Who is like unto thee, O Lord, among the gods? who is like thee, glorious in holiness, fearful in praises, doing wonders? Ex. xv. 11. "Now I know that the Lord is greater than all gods: for in the thing wherein they dwelt proudly he was above them." Ex. xviii. 11. "O Lord God, thou hast begun to shew thy servant thy greatness, and thy mighty hand: for what god is there in heaven or in earth, that can do according to thy works, and according to thy might?" Deut. iii. 24. "For great is the Lord, and greatly to be praised: he also is to be feared above all gods." I. Chron. xvi. 25. "The king answered unto Daniel, and said, Of a truth it is, that your God is a God of gods, and a Lord of kings, and a revealer of secrets." Dan. ii. 47.

2. *Compared with men.* "For my thoughts are not your thoughts, neither are your ways my ways, saith the Lord. For as the heavens are higher than the earth, so are my ways higher than your ways, and my thoughts than your thoughts." Is. lv. 8, 9. "Who would not fear thee, O King of nations? for to thee doth it appertain: forasmuch

as among all the wise men of the nations, and in all their kingdoms, there is none like unto thee." Jer. x. 7. Zech. viii. 6; Ps. l. 21; Job xxxiii. 12.

3. *Eternity of God.* "The eternal God is thy refuge, and underneath are the everlasting arms: and he shall thrust out the enemy from before thee; and shall say, Destroy them." Deut. xxxiii. 27. "Before the mountains were brought forth, or ever thou hadst formed the earth and the world, even from everlasting to everlasting, thou art God." Ps. xc. 2. Is. xli. 4; Jer. x. 10.

4. *His omnipotence.* "Ah Lord God! behold, thou hast made the heaven and the earth by thy great power and stretched-out arms, and there is nothing too hard for thee." Jer. xxxii. 17. "Behold, I am the Lord, the God of all flesh: is there anything too hard for me?" Jer. xxxii. 27. "Whatsoever the Lord pleased, that did he in heaven, and in earth, in the seas, and all deep places." Ps. cxxxv. 6. Rev. xix. 6: Eph. iii. 20.

5. *Omnipresence of God.* "Can any hide himhimself in secret places that I shall not see him? saith the Lord. Do not I fill heaven and earth? saith the Lord." Jer. xxiii. 24. "For his eyes are upon the ways of man, and he seeth all his goings." Job xxxiv. 21. "Thou knowest my down-sitting and mine uprising; thou understandest my thought afar off." Ps. cxxxix. 2. "That

SCIPTURE VIEW OF GOD. 71

they should seek the Lord, if haply they might feel after him, and find him, though he be not far from every one of us." Acts xvii. 27. Ps. cxxxix. 7–10.

6. *The wisdom of God.* "With him is wisdom and strength, he hath counsel and understanding." Job xii. 13. "He that chastiseth the heathen, shall not he correct? he that teacheth man knowledge, shall not he know?" Ps. xciv. 10. Rom. xvi. 25; Jude 25.

7. *Holiness of God.* "Let them praise thy great and terrible name; for it is holy. Exalt ye the Lord our God, and worship at his footstool; for he is holy." Ps. xcix. 3–5. "And one cried unto another, and said, Holy, holy, holy, is the Lord of hosts: the whole earth is full of his glory." Is. vi. 3. I. Sam. ii. 2; James i. 13; Rev. iv. 8.

8. *Justice of God.* "He is the Rock, his work is perfect; for all his ways are judgment: a God of truth and without iniquity, just and right is he." Deut. xxxii. 4. "Justice and judgment are the habitation of thy throne: mercy and truth shall go before thy face." Ps. lxxxix. 14. Ezek. xviii. 29; Rom. ii. 2.

9. *Impartiality of God.* "Behold, God is mighty, and despiseth not any: he is mighty in strength and wisdom." Job xxxvi. 5. "Who will render to every man according to his deeds."

Rom. ii. 6. "Of a truth I perceive that God is no respecter of persons." Acts x. 34. Gal. ii. 6; Eph. vi. 8; Col. iii. 25.

10. *Goodness of God.* "O give thanks unto the Lord: for he is good; for his mercy endureth forever." I. Chron. xvi. 34. "O taste and see that the Lord is good." Ps. xxxiv. 8. "They shall abundantly utter the memory of thy great goodness, and shall sing of thy righteousness. * * * The Lord is good to all; and his tender mercies are over all his works." Ps. cxlv. 7–9. Neh. i. 7; Matt. v. 45.

11. *Mercy and compassion of God.* "For the Lord thy God is a merciful God: he will not forsake thee, neither destroy thee." Deut. iv. 31. "Also unto thee, O Lord, belongeth mercy: for thou renderest to every man according to his work." Ps. lxii. 12. Lam. iii. 22; Dan. ix. 9.

12. *Long-suffering of God.* "But thou, O Lord, art a God full of compassion, and gracious, longsuffering, and plenteous in mercy and truth." Ps. lxxxvi. 15. "And the Lord passed by before him, and proclaimed, The Lord, the Lord God, merciful and gracious, long-suffering, and abundant in goodness." Ex. xxxiv. 6.

With such exalted views of the Divine Being, as expressed in these passages, it is not difficult to conceive how the sacred writers could reverence and adore him. Just, wise, impartial, merciful, long-suffering, good, holy, and compassionate; high above all, nobler than lords, more loving and kind than parents was the Being whom they worshiped. How vastly different the views thus expressed from the notions of the pagan philosophers. Then, too, every Christian has a right to feel and say that "this God is our God forever and ever;" that "their rock is not as our rock, even our enemies themselves being judges."

The heathen worshiped the whole universe taken together, and also in its parts. They thought it unbecoming to worship some of the more eminent parts of that which they regarded as God. They theologized every part and particle of creation, and thought that he might be worshiped in anything. Dr. Cudworth produces a passage from Pliny, which he translates thus: "Frail and toilsome mortality has thus broken and crumbled the Deity into parts, mindful of its own infirmity, that so every one, by parcels and pieces, might worship that in God which himself stands most in need of."

How strangely this sounds when contrasted with those beautiful and exalted utterances of the sacred writers. For these clearer and better views of the being and attributes of God we are indebted to the Bible. But for this divine revelation we would be wandering in the mazes of superstition and ignorance. The Bible, O blessed book, "it is a rock of diamonds, a chain of pearls." The "spirit of the book has ransacked creation to lay its treasures on Jehovah's altar, united the innumerable rays of a far-streaming glory on the little hill of Calvary, and woven a garland for the bleeding brow of Emmanuel, the flowers of which have been culled from the garden of a universe." "I must confess," says the infidel Rousseau, "that the majesty of the Scriptures astonishes me; the holiness of the evangelists speaks to my heart, and has such strong and striking characters of truth, and is, moreover, so perfectly inimitable, that if it had been the invention of men, the invention would be greater than the greatest heroes." Sir Isaac Newton said: "We account the Scriptures of God to be the most sublime philosophy."

"Hast thou ever heard
Of such a book? the author God himself;
The subject, God and man, salvation, life,
And death—eternal life—eternal death."

"Within this ample volume lies
   The mystery of mysteries;
   Happiest they of human race
   To whom their God has given grace,
   To read, to fear, to hope, to pray,
   To lift the latch, to force the way
   And better had he ne'er been born,
   Who reads to doubt, or reads to scorn."

CHAPTER IV.

PROVIDENCE, ITS NATURE AND REASONABLENESS. SCRIPTURE VIEW OF IT.

Providence is a manifestation of that universal superintendence which God exercises over all his creatures. It implies more than forethought: it implies the constant operation of God, subsequent to creation; that he pervades the entire universe, and acts upon every particle of matter, and that he is concerned about every living thing, from the smallest insect to the highest order of intelligent beings. "By him all things consist," and "in him we live, move, and have our being." It is a vast and profound scheme by which the wise purposes of the Almighty are carried forward. Complicated and inexplicable as many of its operations may seem, the final result will be sublime and glorious "God is the soul of providence."

> "He is his own interpreter,
> And he will make it plain."

"Providence is like the ocean—an apt and beautiful allusion. The ocean, broken only here and there by a few large patches of land, sitting, as it were, on its heaving bosom, stretches from pole to pole, and from equator to equator; is all-pervading, never at rest. * * * And such is providence—a deep, unfathomable deep—none but the omniscient eye can fathom it—none but infinite wisdom can scan its secret recesses; so boundless, everywhere active, all-influential, that none but the infinite mind can survey and comprehend its wonder-working operations. Like the sea, providence has i s flows and ebbs, its calms and tempests, its depressions and elevations." But there is not a wave of the sea that breaks along its rocky shore, nor a gentle swell that moves upon its bosom, that has not its purposes, its connections, and its end. So in providence, there is not a motion, however insignificant it may appear, but has its connections, its aim, and end to accomplish.

"The uniform doctrine of the sacred writings is, that throughout the universe nothing happens without God; that his hand is ever active, and his decree of performance or sufferance intervenes in in all; that nothing is too great or unwieldy for his management, and nothing so minute and inconsiderable as to be below his inspection and care. While he is guiding the sun, moon, and stars in their courses through the heavens, and while in this world he is ruling among empires, kingdoms, and republics, turning and overturning the designs and purposes of the great among men, and while he is stilling the raging of the waters, he is at the same time watching over the humble good man, who, in the obscurity of his cottage, is serving and worshiping him."

That we may exhibit more fully, and at the same time more authoritatively, the nature of God's providence, we will refer directly to the word of God. Good men and women are always most concerned to know what God has said. They will listen to men while they weave out fine and beautiful theories, but when done are not satisfied unless it can be shown that God has said so. One word from God has more influence over a good man's heart than a thousand words uttered by men. When God told Abraham to leave his native land and go out into a strange country, immediately he obeyed and went out, not knowing whither he went. With Abraham the command of God was supreme. So with a genuine Christian the word of God will stand, though it should prove every man a liar. Let us then take a scriptural view of the doctrine of providence.

God is the creator and preserver of all things. "Thy righteousness is like the great mountains; thy judgments are a great deep: O Lord, thou preservest man and beast." Ps. xxxvi. 6. "Thou, even thou, art Lord alone: thou hast made heaven, the heaven of heavens, with all their host, the earth, and all things that are therein, the seas, and all that is therein, and thou preservest them all." Neh. ix. 6.

He careth even for animals. "He giveth to the beast his food, and to the young raven which cry." Ps. cxlvii. 9. "Behold the fowls of the air: for they sow not, neither do they reap, nor gather into barns; yet your heavenly Father feedeth them. Are ye not much better than they?" Matt. vi. 26. Ps. civ. 20, 21.

The whole course of nature in all its parts and forces is controlled by him. "While the earth remaineth, seed-time and harvest, and cold and heat, and summer and winter, and day and night shall not cease." Gen. viii. 22. "Thou hast set all the borders of the earth: thou hast made summer and winter." Ps. lxxiv. 17. "Nevertheless he left not himself without witness, in that he did good, and gave us rain from heaven, and fruitful seasons, filling our hearts with food and gladness." Acts xiv. 17.

God preserves and sustains the human race "What shall I do unto thee, O thou preserver of men?" Job vii. 20. "Thou hast granted me life and favor, and thy visitation hath preserved my spirit." Job x. 12. "Behold, he that keepeth Israel shall neither slumber nor sleep. The Lord is thy keeper: the Lord is thy shade upon thy right hand. The Lord shall preserve thy going out and thy coming in from this time forth, and even for evermore." Ps. cxxi. 4, 5, 8. "And even to your old age I am he; and even to hoar hairs will I carry you: I have made, and I will bear; even I will carry, and will deliver you." Is. xlvi. 4.

God is the absolute owner of all things. "Behold, the heaven and the heaven of heavens is the Lord's thy God, the earth also, with all that therein is." Deut. x. 14. "Thine, O Lord, is the greatness, and the power, and the glory, and the victory, and the majesty: for all that is in the heaven and in the earth is thine." I. Chron. xxix. 11. "The earth is the Lord's and the fullness thereof; the world, and they that dwell therein." Ps. xxiv. 1.

God is not only the preserver of man, but the owner of him. "Know ye that the Lord he is God: it is he that hath made us, and not we ourselves; we are his people, and the sheep of his pasture." Ps. c. 3. "For whether we live, we live unto the Lord; and whether we die, we die unto the Lord: whether we live therefore, or die, we are the Lord's." Rom. xiv. 8. "Behold, all souls are mine; as the soul of the father, so also the soul of the son is mine: the soul that sinneth, it shall die." Ezek. xviii. 4.

He controls the temporal affairs of men. "Both

riches and honor come of thee, and thou reignest over all; and in thine hand is power and might; and in thine hand it is to make great, and to give strength unto all." I. Chron. xxix. 12. "But the very hairs of your head are all numbered." Matt. x. 30. "Are not five sparrows sold for two farthings, and not one of them is forgotten before God?" Luke xii. 6.

From these, and a thousand other passages bearing on the same subject, it is evident that God's providence extends to everything. While it is true that we can not account for every phenomenon in nature, nor explain precisely how God influences the thoughts, designs, and will of man, and at the same time leaves him to the freedom of his own choice,—nor can we tell how nor why he often leads him into dark and mysterious paths,—yet the fact of an overruling power or influence is so clearly set forth in the word of God, and so constantly experienced in our lives, that we are not at liberty to call it in question. Neither is it necessary for us to understand all the ways and purposes of the Almighty. The nature of that secret by which he directs the planets in their course is all a mystery to us, and yet we know that he does it.

> "That things to mortals are mysterious,
> Is not because the things themselves are dark,
> But the perceptions through which they are viewed."

Everything in the universe, from the highest order of intelligences down to the smallest insect that lives but an hour, is under the immediate supervision and control of the Almighty. If he moves the heavenly bodies, causes the winds to blow, the rains to fall, the grass to grow, the ocean to ebb and flow, and the earth to quake by established laws, no matter. God is the soul of every law, whether it be mental, physical, or moral. If his presence and power were withdrawn, every law in the universe would fall flexible as the lash of a whip, and creation would run wild. "The primary cause of things must certainly be some powers and principles not mechanical." The philosopher, says an excellent writer, who overlooks the laws of an all-governing deity in nature, contents himself with the appearance of the material universe only, and the mechanical laws of motion, neglects what is most excellent, and prefers what is imperfect to what is supremely perfect, finitude to infinity, what is narrow and weak to what is unlimited and almighty, and what is perishing to what endures forever. Sir Isaac Newton thought it most unaccountable to exclude the Deity out of the universe. To him it appeared far more just and reasonable to suppose that the whole chain of causes, or the several series of them, should center in God as their source, and the whole system to depend on him as the only independent cause. Any other conclusion is most absurd and unreasonable.

The doctrine of providence may be most successfully argued from a consideration of the divine perfections. It is his right to govern and control all things, material and immaterial, "whose attributes, physical and moral, best qualify him to secure the end of government." God is all-powerful, all-wise, just, benevolent, and everywhere present, and is therefore in every way qualified to govern. To illustrate: there reposes deep in the human soul the full consciousness that we are responsible to some superior being for our conduct. No matter how we reason to the contrary, we can not get away from this consciousness. To whom does right reason say we should be responsible? To this question there can be but one answer. Both reason and revelation unite in saying that the Creator of all things should be the judge of the earth. Why? From him we derive our being, and his natural attributes, moral perfections, and necessary relation to man and the universe, point him out as the only being who has a right to govern, and the only being that is capable to govern all things. "If God is not a moral governor, our very nature deceives us; and the whole universe, so far as we have the means of knowing it, is calculated to mislead mankind in respect to this fundamental truth."

Because we see traces of design in all the works of nature, does it necessarily follow that the designer is in no other way connected with it, only as its creator? By what process of reasoning can we justly come to that conclusion? Now, when we see these marks of design we say, and properly too, that there must have been a designing mind as the author. But surely we are not by this compelled to believe that the Almighty Creator was only the first link in the chain, while every subsequent link has been added by chance. Is it not far more reasonable to expect the presence of the designer wherever we behold such striking evidences of design? Why should men be so anxious to rid the universe of its Creator? Are the affairs of creation safer under the control of chance than under the management of a wise, merciful, and benevolent God?

It is a wicked and ungrateful reflection upon the divine character to say that he is or can be indifferent toward any of his works. God is everywhere present, and sees everything that transpires, even to the falling of a sparrow, and can, without the slightest shadow of difficulty, do any good that his wisdom and benevolence dictate. God can not withdraw his presence from any part of his works. If he did he would cease to be God, for omnipresence is an essential attribute of his nature.

> "God hath a presence, and that ye may see
> In the fold of the flower, the leaf of the tree,
> In the sun of the noonday, the star of the night,
> In the storm-cloud of darkness, the rain-bow of light,
> In the waves of the ocean, the furrows of land,
> In the mountains of granite, the atoms of sand,
> Turn where ye may, from the sky to the sod,
> Where can you gaze that ye see not God?"

To farther demonstrate the truth of what we have stated, we will again turn to the Holy Scriptures, and from them show that whatever occurs on earth and among men is not independent of God, but by his direction or permission. The whole course of nature, from first to last, is maintained by him, as the word of God most abundantly testifies. There is no source from which a Christian can draw greater consolation than this: God is everywhere controlling and superintending the works of his own hands.

Day and night are controlled by him. "Which commandeth the sun, and it riseth not, and sealeth up the stars." Job ix. 7. "Canst thou bring forth Mazzaroth in his season? or canst thou guide Arcturus with his sons?" Job xxxviii. 32. "Thus saith the Lord, which giveth the sun for a light by day, and the ordinances of the moon and of the stars for a light by night." Jer. xxxi 35.

He controls the rain and causeth it to fall. "Who giveth rain upon the earth, and sendeth water upon the fields." Job v. 10. "Thou visitest the earth, and waterest it: thou greatly enrichest it with the river of God, which is full of water: thou preparest them corn, when thou hast so provided for it." Ps. lxv. 9. "He watereth the hills from his chambers: the earth is satisfied with the fruit of thy works." Ps. civ. 13. "He causeth the vapors to ascend from the ends of the earth; he maketh lightnings for the rain; he bringeth the wind out of his treasuries." Ps. cxxxv. 7.

The clouds, hail, cold, and snow are maintained and controlled by him. "He bindeth up the waters in his thick clouds; and the cloud is not rent under them." Job xxvi. 8. "Also by watering he wearieth the thick cloud: he scattereth his bright cloud: and it is turned round about by his counsels: that they may do whatsoever he commandeth them upon the face of the world in the earth." Job. xxxvii. 11, 12. "For he saith to the snow, Be thou on the earth; likewise to the small rain, and to the great rain of his strength. * * * By the breath of God frost is given: and the breadth of the waters is straitened." Job. xxxvii. 6, 10. "He giveth snow like wool: he scattereth the hoar-frost like ashes. He casteth forth his ice like morsels: who can stand before his cold?" Ps. cxlvii. 16, 17.

The thunder, lightnings, and wind are maintained by him. "The Lord thundered from heaven, and the Most High uttered his voice." II. Sam. xxii. 14. "God thundereth marvelously with his voice; great things doth he, which we can not comprehend." Job xxxvii. 5. "The voice of thy thunder was in the heaven: the lightnings lighted the world: the earth trembled and shook." Ps. lxxvii. 18. "For he looketh to the ends of the earth, and seeth under the whole heaven; to make the weight for the winds: and he weigheth the waters by measure." Job. xxviii. 24, 25. "He sendeth out his word and melteth them: he causeth his wind to blow, and the waters flow." Ps. cxlvii. 18.

We have been thus particular in giving these several quotations under appropriate heads, to show in the clearest possible light that God is not only connected with the universe as its Creator, but is at all times everywhere present, maintaining the course of nature. In the passages given it is said plainly and positively that he controls everything. The seasons, day and night, rain, clouds, hail, snow, cold, the thunders and lightnings, are all maintained and moved by his invisible power. We may not understand precisely how he operates in nature, nor is it essential to our present or future happiness that we should know. We know that in the beginning God created the heavens and the earth. How he did it we may not know: but we know that all things were made by him. So in the operations of his providences, while we are not permitted to see the hand that moves the world and superintends the falling of a sparrow, as also the penciling of a flower, yet we know the hand is there.

If it be said that God, when he created the universe, set everything in motion, and connected with it certain immutable laws by which all things in nature were to be governed, and that he then left it without farther care or concern, we answer that whilst we may not be able to reason well on a subject of such a nature, yet it would certainly appear most unaccountable that a wise and benevolent Creator should have so arranged his works in nature as not to allow himself "room for his own continued action." Then, also, it would argue that when he completed his work, and set things in motion, he ceased to care for it. But the scriptures we have quoted declare most plainly that his presence and action are continued in all the operations and developments of nature. There is not a law in the universe, whether it be mental, moral, or physical, but would at once be rendered inoperative if the presence and power of God were withdrawn.

But "there are narrow minds which can never take in more than one truth. Because natural law universally prevails, they would exclude everything but natural law;" they would banish the Creator from his own creation, and invest those laws with the very attributes which belong to God, and to him only; they would rather worship the creature than the creator. They reverence the law, but set at naught the lawgiver; forgetting, as it would seem, that it would be most unreasonable and unnatural for a wise and benevolent Creator to forget or become indifferent to the works of his own hands.

We have seen thus far that God maintains and superintends the usual course of nature; that all the forces in the universe are under his control; that nothing does or can transpire in nature without his action. We wish now to invite particular attention to another point, which in many respects is closely allied to what we have said. We have seen how God's providence reaches out into every possible department of nature; we will, next in order, see how the human race is affected by it. Here, as in our previous remarks, we will be guided in our thoughts by the word of God. And may we not hope that the Holy Spirit will so enlighten our minds and open the Scriptures to our understanding that we may see and feel our relation to God, and also our responsibility to him.

God's providences to mankind in general. "Both riches and honor come of thee, and thou reignest over all; and in thine hand is power and might; and in thine hand is to make great, and to give strength unto all." I. Chron. xxix. 12. "But who am I, and what is my people, that we should be able to offer so willingly after this sort? for all things come of thee, and of thine own have we given thee." I. Chron. xxix. 14 "Are not five sparrows sold for two farthings, and not one of them is forgotten before God? But even the very hairs of your head are all numbered. Fear not therefore: ye are of more value than many sparrows." Luke xii. 6, 7.

God overrules the designs and purposes of men. "Now therefore be not grieved, nor angry with yourselves, that ye sold me hither: for God did send me before you to preserve life. And God sent me before you to preserve you a posterity. So now it was not you that sent me hither, but God: and he hath made me a father to Pharaoh, and lord over all his house. * * * But as for you, ye thought evil against me; but God meant it unto good, to bring to pass, as it is this day, to save much people alive." Gen. xlv. 5, 7, 8; 1. 20. "There are many devices in a man's heart; nevertheless the counsel of the Lord, that shall stand." Prov. xix. 21. "O Lord, I know that the way of man is not in himself: it is not in man that walketh to direct his steps." Jer. x. 23.

Human efforts are vain without God. "Except the Lord build the house, they labor in vain that build it: except the Lord keep the city, the watchman waketh but in vain. It is vain for you to rise up early, to sit up late, to eat the bread of sorrows: for so he giveth his beloved sleep." Ps. cxxvii. 1, 2. "Behold, is it not of the Lord of hosts that the people shall labor in the very fire, and the people shall weary themselves for very vanity." Hab. ii. 13.

All temporal supplies come from God. "And he will love thee, and bless thee, and multiply thee: he will also bless the fruit of thy womb, and the fruit of thy land, thy corn, and thy wine, and thine oil, the increase of thy kine, and the flocks of thy sheep, in the land which he sware unto thy fathers to give thee." Deut. vii. 13. " O Lord our God, all this store that we have prepared to build thee a house for thine holy name cometh of thine hand, and is all thine own." I. Chr. xxix. 16.

Change fo fortune is from God. He gives prosperity, protection, and sends adversity. "The Lord killeth, and maketh alive: he bringeth down to the grave, and bringeth up. The Lord maketh poor, and maketh rich: he bringeth low, and lifteth up. He raiseth up the poor out of the dust, and lifteth up the beggar from the dunghill, to set them among princes, and to make them inherit the throne of glory." 1. Sam. ii. 6–8. "He hath put down the mighty from their seats, and exalted them of low degree." Luke i. 52. "It is God that girdeth me with strength, and maketh my way perfect. He maketh my feet like hinds' feet, and setteth me upon my high places." Ps. xviii. 32, 33. "He will surely violently turn and toss thee like a ball into a large country: there shalt thou die, and there the chariots of thy glory shall be the shame of thy lord's house." Is. xxi. 18.

From these passages, which we preferred to give without comment, we are taught as plainly as language can teach that God directs or overrules everything that relates to man's temporal concerns. He can raise up and put down, kill and make alive, give or withhold prosperity, give protection or send adversity, can make rich or make poor, and withal never interferes with the moral agency of man. What he orders he controls, and what he permits he overrules, so that there is no conflict between his sovereignty and man's responsibility. As God is immediately connected with his own works in the material universe, so he is directly connected with man. His care and general supervision are manifest in the growing lily, the spire of grass, and the forming of a leaf, and in like manner in relation to man, mentally, morally, and physically. A sparrow doth not fall without his notice, and he has numbered the hairs of our heads.

Those who are so greatly concerned to make it appear that all things are governed by fixed laws should remember that this view does not necessarily exclude the Creator from his own creation. He can do as he pleases. He might have governed and controlled everything without any established laws, or he might have so constituted the universe that there should have been only a few general laws, and have made it much less complicated in its general arrangements. Nevertheless, there are wise purposes served by this complication. It gives a variety to the works of God, by which he is able to accomplish individual and general ends. "By this means," says Dr. McCosh, "he can produce effects which could not have followed from the operations of the laws acting; and by this means human foresight is lessened, human power controlled, and man rendered dependent on his Maker."

> "Sad error, this, to take
> The light of nature rather than the light
> Of revelation for a guide. As well
> Prefer the borrowed light of earth's pale moon
> To the effulgence of the noonday sun."

There is in the true idea of a providence a perfect foresight into everything, and a wise and gracious provision for everything. God in his wisdom foresaw and by his power provided for everything, so that all things, material and immaterial, must be dependent upon him. He might operate in nature without law. He chose instead to work by law or by second causes; but in either case he must be present to superintend in everything, whether relating to physical or spiritual existence. And this view, as we have seen, the word of God most abundantly establishes. To prevent any misconception upon this important point I will state again, that although God has chosen to govern and control all things by certain established laws or second causes, yet those laws are all dependent upon him for their power. If God's presence were withdrawn, every law and every force in nature would cease to operate, and the whole universe would instantly be thrown into wild confusion.

> "Thou teachest not a leaf can grow,
> Till life from thee within it flow;
> That not a speck of dust can be,
> O Fount of Being, save by thee."

In Tucker's "Light of Nature" there are some most excellent thoughts bearing upon this subject, which we will here insert. "Therefore," says this writer, "let not men condemn one another too hastily of impiety or superstition, for both are relative to the strength of each person's sight. The philosopher may entertain so high an opinion of infinite wisdom, as that upon the formation of a world it might provide for every event that is to happen during the whole period of its continuance; therefore he is not impious in asserting that all things since have gone on in the course of natural causes, for his idea of the first is so full as to leave no room for anything to be interposed. This the plain man can not comprehend, the lines of his view being short; therefore he is not superstitious in imagining frequent interpositions, because without them he can not understand a providence at all. He may likewise find it impossible to conceive that every motion of matter and turn of volition should be calculated or foreseen, but supposes a watchful providence continually attentive to the tendency of second causes interposing every hour and day to correct the errors of chance, and secretly turning the springs of action the way that wisdom and goodness recommend. And he is excusable therein, if this be the best conception he can form; for it derogates not from his idea of the Divine wisdom and dominion to imagine that there should be room left in nature for chance, so long as there is a superintending power who can foresee the irregularities of chance, in time enough to prevent them. Thus, how largely soever we may ascribe to interposition, or how much soever deduct therefrom to add to the disposing providence, we can not deny that every natural cause we see is an effect of some prior cause, impulse of impulse, and volition of motives and ideas suggested to the mind, therefore must refer all dispositions ultimately to the act of God; and as we can not imagine him to act without knowing what he does, and what will result therefrom, we must conclude that act to proceed upon a plan and disposition of the causes tending to produce the particular consequence following therefrom. The only difference between the man of common sense and the studious is concerning the time the disposition was made, which the one thinks a few days or a few minutes, the other many ages ago; the one frequent and occasional, the other rare and universal; but both acknowledge that nothing ever happens without the permission of one Almighty and ever-vigilant Governor."

It can not be of any possible advantage to our reverence for the divine character to suppose that there are frequent or occasional interpositions, independent of physical causes, except so far as miracles were necessary to attest the truth of divine revelation. The whole machinery of nature is so complete and perfect in all its arrangements, that there can be no demand for special interpositions. In the original disposition of the several parts of this vast machinery, everything was so wisely arranged and adjusted, as not to require change. "This is in fact the great miracle of providence, that no miracles are needed to accomplish its purposes."

There is exhibited in the works of God a most perfect harmony, which is not the result of any special interpositions, but comes from a wise prearrangement. This does not, however, separate God from the government of all things. it only establishes the fact that he had the wisdom to foresee everything, and the power and goodness to provide for everything; and except so far as it may have been necessary to establish the truth of a divine revelation by miracle, there have been no interferences with the laws of nature. What God does is in harmony with established laws. He foresaw what would be necessary, and provided for it. There are no new laws or forces created for special emergencies. There may be effects produced that are strange and mysterious to us, but it is presumable that there are hidden laws and forces in nature which the researches of science have not yet discovered. These laws and forces in nature were all ordained of God, and are subject to his will. "If we see God in any one part of his works we must, for a like reason, see him in every other part. If we exclude him from any part, we must, for a like reason, exclude him from all." But as we have seen, the Bible ascribes every effect to God. He sends the rain, heat, cold, snow, controls the wind, thunders, and lightnings, guides the sun, moon. and stars, causes the earth to produce whatever is necessary to sustain life. All this is done through the agency of established laws or second causes.

> "O vain philosophy, thou wandering light
> Which hast so oft misled our steps, attend!
> And, prostrate at this heavenly shrine, lament
> Thy blindness, and forego thy pride; here cast
> Thy trophies down, undeck thyself of all
> Thy borrowed plumes, and own the Fountain whence
> Thy hoary sons recieved the living fire,
> Which animates the glowing page they penned."

CHAPTER V.

PROVIDENCE, PARTICULAR AND GENERAL

"God, providence—an after life,
Here is firm footing—this is sol'' 'ick.
This can sustain us—all is sea beside."

There are and have been different and conflicting opinions among some of the wisest and best men respecting the nature of God's providences, whether it is particular or general. This distinction, whether real or only apparent, does not necessarily imply an antagonism between the doctrines or opinions themselves. It does, however, demonstrate the truth of Paul's declaration, when he said that "now we see through a glass darkly." "We see in part and understand in part." No man, however learned, can boast of understanding all there is in any one truth. We see everything that we see at all "through a glass darkly." Most truth we do not see at all. One man sees a fragment of some great truth, another man equally learned and sincere, sees another fragment. They are not opposites, but fragments of the same truth, or truth viewed from different stand-points. A traveler in a distant land states that two friends who were in company with him happened to be standing on opposite sides of a tree, and they entered into a sharp dispute about the color of the leaves. One said they were green, and the other said they were white. Now, the leaves were green on the upper surface and pure silvery white on the under surface. The wind was blowing from the face of the one directly into the face of the other, so that the under part of the leaf was turned to one, and the upper surface was turned to the other. They disputed and contended until a third party, who had been quietly looking on, interfered. when they discovered that they were both right and both wrong. The difficulty was owing to the different points from which they viewed the same object. Thus men often see Bible truths from different points of view. One man sees one part of a truth, and another man sees another fragment of the same truth. Now, they may both be correct, only they can not see how to put these fragments together. One says that providence is general, and another says it is particular and special. Now, I conceive that both are right; for "the general providence of God, properly understood, reaches to the most particular and minute objects and events, and the particular providence of God becomes general by its embracing every particular."

Either of these opinions taken separately, is incorrect, for it limits the power, wisdom, and goodness of God. Those who contend for a general providence only see God's operations very much as they see their own. They, in contemplating important events, must necessarily overlook a great many minor matters; so they imagine God, in providing for and managing the affairs of the universe, takes cognizance only of the general plans and events, leaving all minor incidents to take care of themselves, or to be provided for as they come up. They bring God within the prescribed and narrow limits of man's methods, as though he were "altogether such a one as themselves." This view of the subject implies that God is not capable of knowing what may occur, or indifferent as to the results that may follow. But God's providential government, whilst it includes the care and oversight of empires and kingdoms, extends as well to the sparrow and the lily. "The pains, if we may so speak, which God has taken to beautify every leaf and flower,—nay, every weed which we trample under foot,—the new beauties unseen by the naked eye, which the microscope discloses in the vegetable kingdom, and the beautiful organization of the insect world, all show that the greatness of God is peculiarly seen in the care which he takes of objects the most minute." "In the government of this world, the individual is not lost in the general on the one hand, nor is the general neglected in the attention to the individual on the other hand. No creature, no object, however insignificant, has been overlooked. The general includes every individual, which finds accordingly its appropriate place. Provision has been made for all and for each in the grand system of the universe."

It is not within the power of man to understand all the ways and purposes of God. For as the heavens are high above the earth, so are his ways and purposes high above man's ways and plans. Man is weak, ignorant, and selfish; while God is wise, powerful, and benevolent. There is an all-wise and skillful arrangement of the laws and forces in nature by which all things are controlled. The word providence implies not only foresight, but timely care, so that ample provision is made for future use and application. God does not change any of his laws to meet particular cases, for they were so wisely adjusted in the beginning as not to require a change, and yet so as to meet every case, and accomplish all his purposes, so that his providence becomes general, because it embraces every particular, and it becomes particular because it embraces everything in general. Hence the idea of special interpositions can not be accepted, except in cases when a miracle was intended.

A great deal has been said and written at one time and another about special providences, or special interpositions; and there are many events in life which, to our limited understanding and comprehension, have the appearance of special interpositions. But a clear understanding of the doctrine of providence would divorce this idea from the mind. Those manifestations of God's particular care and protection which we are permitted to see, we are wont to call special providences; when, if we could see and understand all that he does and the reason why he does it, we would call them all special. Two eminent divines were once in conversation upon this subject, when one said: "I met with a most wonderful manifestation of providence the other day. I was riding across a very high bridge, and my horse became frightened and almost precipitated me off the bridge. If I had gone over, I certainly would have lost my life." "That," said the other, "was certainly a most gracious providence. Nevertheless, I was favored with a greater manifestation of God's care than even that. It was on this wise: I was riding across that same bridge, and my horse did not scare at all." The one saw a special providence in being delivered when in danger, and the other saw an equally special interposition in not being thrust into danger. Which shall be deemed the greater, to deliver out of danger or to save from being exposed to the danger?

If we were permitted to see and understand all the plans and operations of providence, reaching from the beginning to the end of time, and connected in some way with every incident in human life, we would say it was all special. But we are looking through a glass darkly. We see in part and understand in part. We are permitted to have occasional glimpses of our Father's doings, and they are marvelous in our eyes. Our Father is very kind to his beloved, in permitting them to have these occasional glimpses. But when that which is in part is taken away and we shall be enabled to see as we are seen, we will discover that the Father's hand was with us at all times and in all places; that his eye was ever upon us, and that he was ever concerned for our welfare. I was once upon a train of cars that was thrown from the track, and badly broken up; but no lives were lost. Several persons were more or less injured. When the excitement was over, a number of gentlemen and ladies became enthusiastic in talking about providence,—what a wonderful deliverance, what a special interposition. No one would doubt for a moment the providence of God that saved us, but our deliverance was no more special than keeping the train on the track before and after the accident occured. If the train had not been thrown off, but few if any would have thought of providence at all. God does not change or interpose his laws to meet every case; these have been so wisely arranged as not to require special interposition. It is an overwhelming thought that God foresaw every possible event that would transpire in the universe. He is never taken by surprise, but seeing the end from the beginning he has wisely adjusted all the laws and forces in nature, so that events are managed and controlled in a manner so as not to interfere with his sovereignty nor the moral agency of man.

A great error is committed by some divines in supposing that prophecies produced certain great events, whereas the events produced the prophecies. It was predicted that Jerusalem should be destroyed, and it was so; but it was not destroyed on account of the prophecy. God foresaw what would be, and hence the prediction. So in providence, God foresaw everything that would occur, and hence provided for it, not by creating new laws and forces to meet every particular case, but by controlling the powers that be.

Dr. McCosh says: "We do not expect Etna to recall her fires when a sage is near, or the air and ocean to acquire new motions to preserve a saint from danger; for if the sage has been contending with the laws which he professes to observe, or if the saint has been despising what he should regard as the 'ordinances of heaven,' it may be the will of God that these very powers should be the means of destroying him. But should these individuals not be rushing against the known laws of heaven, or should it be the will of God to preserve them, it will be found that provision has been made for their escape, and that not through the powers of nature's own laws, but through other powers in nature opportunely interposing to stop, to turn aside, or otherwise to modify their operations."

> "Think we, like some weak prince, the Eternal Cause
> Prone for his favorites to reverse his laws?
> Shall burning Etna, if a sage requires,
> Forget to thunder, or recall her fires?
> On air or sea new motions be impressed,
> Oh, blameless Bethel, to relieve thy hest;
> When the loose mountains tumble from on high
> Shall gravitation cease if you go by?"

The Stoics believed that providence only superintended or controlled great events; that it was inconsistent with the ease and dignity of the divine character to trouble himself about the ordinary occurrences of life. Balbus, who was a leading man among the Stoics, in speaking of divine providence, said: "The gods take care of great matters and neglect small ones." Unfortunately, there are many Christians who have fallen into the notions of Balbus. They see no providence except in extraordinary matters. They see no beauty in that scripture which teaches them to "cast all their care upon him," nor do they feel any comfort in the assurance given, that he careth for them. Providence as certainly means to supply the wants of all as to rule over all. And he is the happier man who can see God in the small as well as the great events of life.

Every effort that is made to discriminate between a particular and general providence only leads to distrust and confusion. If we say that God superintends one class of events and not another, we necessarily represent him as being weak and partial. In a watch there is a number of wheels, posts, and pins. If one of these is misplaced the instrument will not keep time. The watch-maker must see that each has its proper place. If he would devote all his attention to the proper adjustment of some of the larger wheels, and neglect some of the smaller ones, the whole machine would be defective and worthless. So God, in managing the affairs of the universe, must see that every wheel, post, and pin is in the right place. God is as much present when the tiny spire of grass is formed, as when the earth is shaken by an earthquake. The laws and forces in nature by which the slightest tint in the petal of a flower is produced, must be superintended and directed with as much care as those by which the planets are kept in their courses. The providence of God is just as special in supporting and caring for the infant in the cradle as it is when that infant has grown to be a man and governs an empire or a kingdom. The former, stoicism passes unnoticed, while the latter is set down as an exhibition of special care and concern.

But these visible and more striking manifestations of the care of God are well enough, for if they were not brought thus to our notice we would soon forget that he takes any care of us at all. They serve to remind us that he is working, and that we ought to recognize his hand in everything, however insignificant it may seem to us. How clearly and beautifully this lesson is taught us in the Bible. "A sparrow shall not fall without his notice," and the hairs of our head are numbered. This, we say, is a very small matter,—and so it is, comparatively,—nevertheless, it is of sufficient importance to be noticed by the Father of us all. "All things," says Dr. Clarke, "are ordained by the counsel of God. * * * Nothing escapes his merciful regards."

> "He sees with equal eyes, as God of all,
> A hero perish, and a sparrow fall."

This doctrine of an all-wise, all-pervading, and impartial providence brings to the weary, sad heart and trembling faith a most glorious consolation. While the world goes on praising a providence that has overturned a kingdom and shaken an empire, the humble, trusting Christian in his out-of-the-way cottage can say that "the same hand prepares my steps and controls events about me with as much care and tenderness as though I were the only person in the universe." John, on the lonely isle of Patmos, could draw real heart-comfort from the thought that God is everywhere, and that his hand controls every event.

> "There is a Power
> Unseen that rules the illimitable world,
> That guides its motions, from the brightest star
> To the least dust of this sin-tainted mold;
> While man, who madly deems himself the lord
> Of all, is naught but weakness and dependence."

No one hesitates to ascribe the ruling and controlling of great events to God. In this there is a pretty general agreement. But a host of men and women—and they may be found among Christian as well as heathen people—practically deny that providence extends to minor matters; and even when it does descend to little things it is treated with indifference. The notion seems to be this, that God takes special pains in managing important matters, and binds the smaller ones into bundles, and casts them about with indifference. All believe that God created the world, but do not seem to conceive that in creating the world he must have created every atom of matter that enters into the whole. It is said that "God hath measured the waters in the hollow of his hand." Could he have measured the waters without measuring the drops of which the ocean is composed? If we say that God preserves man, we necessarily include the idea that all the means and subordinate causes, however small and trifling they may seem to be, were distinctly and particularly embraced in the plan. And farther, that such preservation could not and would not occur if the minutest parts were left out. Now there is in each part that goes to make up the whole as much of a special providence as there is in the whole, when the general plan is consummated. "A house consists of a great number of parts, each of which was included in the design of the architect, and is as much the product of his ingenuity and labor as the building itself. These parts were formed and may exist separately: but in this state they answer no valuable purpose; it is only when brought together and arranged in proper order that they constitute a building. When we affirm that this house was planned by the skill and built by the labor of the architect, may we not affirm, and do we not affirm, that all parts, even down to the minutest, were equally the product of his skill? The building could not exist without the parts, nor could the parts have existed without the design and agency of the builder." So, when we affirm that God created this world we also affirm that he created all the parts of it, even down to the small dust of the balance. And when we affirm that God preserves the lives of men, we as certainly affirm that all the means and subordinate causes, that in any way assisted in his preservation, were arranged and provided by the same Being who preserved the whole. Because we see effects without seeing or understanding the cause, we are not on that account to deny the pre-existence of the cause.

To illustrate still farther. A man is passing through a wood. A limb is broken from a tree and falls to the ground, but he escapes unhurt. Now, there was no miracle wrought in his deliverance; no new laws created; no forces arrested. He was saved from purely natural causes. He heard the limb crack, saw it falling, and sprang to one side. But he says it was a wonderful providence, a special interposition. Providence, as we have said, not only includes foresight, but implies a provision of whatever is necessary. God had provided the man with the sense of hearing, he heard the limb crack; he was provided with the sense of vision, he looked up and saw the limb falling; he was also provided with the power of volition, he sprang to one side and thus escaped. But was there not a providence in his escape? Certainly there was. God had provided him with the necessary means to escape, and was present to sustain those powers. If God had withdrawn his sustaining presence and power, the man would have become deaf, blind, and powerless in an instant, and his escape would have been impossible. God did not change the law of falling bodies, so that the limb changed its course, he only sustained what he had already provided. But if a man should put a lightning-rod on his head and run out into a thunder-storm, he might lose his life. "Etna will not cease to thunder, because a sage goes by."

We see Joseph with his father and brethren in Egypt, where there was abundance to sustain both man and beast, while the famine was all around them. This is most generally set down among the special providences. But look at the long train of events which were made subservient to this great end. We see Joseph hated by his brethren; cast into the dry pit; his dreams; his coat of many colors; sold; in Potiphar's house; in prison and then a ruler. Like the different parts of a building before they are put together, none of them of any particular value in their detached relation, but when properly arranged and fixed in their places forming a beautiful building; so when all the events in the life of Joseph are put together they present a most interesting view of the workings of divine providence. Yet we can not say that any one link in the chain of events was more special than the other. Each event was special, and the whole taken together make up a general providence. God did not order all the incidents in the life of Joseph, but his hand was in it from first to last, controlling and overruling Joseph himself believed this, for he said, after that he was made known to his brethren: "Now therefore be not grieved, nor angry with yourselves, that ye sold me hither: for God did send me before you to preserve life. * * * So now it was not you that sent me hither, but God. * * * But as for you, ye thought evil against me, but God meant it unto good."

No one truth is more clearly demonstrated in the word of God than this, that every effect and every event in the providence of God are so many links in one grand chain, reaching sometimes through many centuries. Divine providence is carried forward by numerous instrumentalities and agencies; but this does not alter the case at all. Because God works through agencies, it by no means excludes him from the work. "These agencies, whether they be rational or irrational creatures, with or without life, are all completely dependent on the Almighty, and could neither exist nor act without his support." A bird could not fly over our head, nor a fish swim in the sea, if it were not sustained by the same hand that guides the moon and stars in their course. God might have so constituted the affairs in the universe that he could have operated upon matter and mind independent of second causes, but he chose to work by instrumentalities.

The preservation of human life does not depend upon one thing alone, but upon the several means employed, and each of these upon other means. Bread, for example, is necessary to sustain human life; but this must be produced, and several instrumentalities must be employed in the process of production. The ground must be cultivated and the seed sown. Then there must be moisture, sunshine, and heat to nourish and promote the growth, until from the first germ of life the full grain is perfected and made ready for the hand of the reaper. All these are links in the chain, and all are necessary to the preservation of human life. But the Scriptures affirm that God preserves human life, and so he does; not by working miracles, but by sustaining and controlling the existing laws and forces in nature, so that the means necessary to the sustenance of life are produced. God exercises a wise and gracious care over the whole human family, and sustains and manages all the laws and forces in nature. If it were not for this all-pervading care the whole universe would be thrown into wild confusion, and man and all other living creatures would instantly perish

>"On God for all events depend;
>You can not want when God's your friend,
>Weigh well your part, and do your best;
>Leave to your Maker all the rest.
>The hand which formed thee in the womb,
>Guides from the cradle to the tomb."

While the Rev. Dr. Rogers lived at St. George's, in the State of Maryland, one of his neighbors determined to take his life. "Accordingly, the miserable wretch made every preparation for executing his nefarious purpose. He watched the motions of Mr. Rogers, with a loaded musket, day after day, for a considerable time, and eagerly sought for a favorable opportunity to destroy his life. He waylaid him when he rode abroad; he hovered about his door at intervals by day and night. But something always occurred to carry the object of his pursuit in a different direction from that which was expected, and thus to avert the intended mischief." But there was no miracle wrought in the preservation of Mr. Rogers' life—no new law created or old one destroyed. Mr. Rogers knew nothing about the intended mischief. But God at the proper time brought into operation all the motives and circumstances that were necessary to save the life of his servant. It was a general providence, and yet every link in the whole chain of incidents was so wisely adjusted that the designed result was secured. No one part of it was any more special than another, because there was a combination of motives and circumstances necessary to accomplish the end. It was a special providence in this, that every link had to be properly adjusted to meet the case. It was a general providence, because it included every link in the whole chain.

When Mr. Rogers was made acquainted with the fact that an attempt had been made to take his life, he regarded the whole as a special interposition of divine providence. But suppose the fact had never been communicated to him, it would have passed without a single thought of special care. Now, life is a very delicate thing, and requires the most constant care to preserve it. We are continually surrounded with dangers, and have doubtless made a thousand hair-breadth escapes, but were not permitted to see the danger to which we were exposed. But when from some eminence in the better land we shall be permitted with clearer vision to look back over life, we shall see that there were ten thousand special providences which we were not permitted to see at the time; we shall see that here and there and yonder the hand of the Lord turned our steps when we were on the very brink of some yawning gulf; and we shall see that all these special interferences were but parts of one grand and glorious plan, and that one operation was just as special as another; and last, but not least, we shall see that providence was always busy and superintending, directing and controlling all affairs.

The pious psalmist, whose spiritual vision was for the most part clear, attributed the preservation of all things to God. "O Lord, thou preservest man and beast." God feedeth the ravens. "Thou openest thine hand, they are filled with good; thou hidest thy face, they are troubled; thou satisfiest the desire of every living thing." But how does God preserve the life of every living thing? The food that is necessary to sustain life is not produced miraculously, but depends upon causes which already exist, and these again on other causes; and thus, if we will, we may go back through effects and causes until we reach the Great First Cause of all things. "We are taught," says an excellent writer, "to pray to our Father in heaven for our *daily bread*. But why pray to him for it, unless its provision depends on his wisdom and care? The causes on which the provision of this bread depends are also ascribed to him. 'And God said, Let the earth bring forth grass, the herb yielding seed, and the fruit-tree yielding fruit after his kind.' Gen. i. 11. 'He maketh his sun to rise on the evil and on the good, and sendeth rain on the just and on the unjust.' Matt. v. 45. If the preservation of our life requires bread, for this bread we are taught to pray, and thus to acknowledge it as one of his blessings. If this bread is produced by other means, these means are instruments in the hand of Omnipotence, employed for this special purpose. All second causes are the servants of the Supreme Ruler, waiting on him in readiness to perform his will."

Everything, animate and inanimate, is sustained and controlled by the providential care of the Almighty. The beasts of the field, the fowls of the air, the fishes of the sea, and the tiny insects that float in the summer air, all creatures small and great, are sustained by him, for "he causeth the grass to grow for the cattle, and the herb for the service of man." He bringeth the wind out of his treasuries; "he causeth his wind to blow.' And when he pleaseth, "he stayeth his rough wind, and gathereth it in his fist." He not only causeth all these things to come to pass, but he pencils every color of the lily, the pink, and the rose, and gives to every leaf and every spire of grass its own shape. "He measures the water in the hollow of his hand; he weigheth the mountains in scales, and the hills in balances." He directeth the lightnings and guides the resistless thunderbolt. God owns all things, and has a right to control all things; and to him are ascribed earthquakes, lightnings and thunder, wind, storms, hail, rain, dew, floods, drought, famine, light, darkness, prosperity, adversity, sickness, health, life, and death. To him therefore should be ascribed honor, majesty, glory, and power; and to him every knee should bow, and before him every tongue should confess, "for his mercy endureth forever."

"Soul of the world, All-seeing Eye,
Where, where shall man thy presence fly?
Say, would he climb the starry hight?
All heaven is instinct with thy light;
Dwell in the darkness of the grave?
Yea, thou art there to judge and save.

In vain on wings of morn we soar,
In vain the realms of space explore,
In vain retreat to shades of night,—
For what can veil us from thy sight?
Distance dissolves before thy ray
And darkness kindles into day."

CHAPTER VI.

PROVIDENCE—UNIVERSAL.

The doctrine of a universal providence rests mainly on the doctrine of the universal presence of God. We have, in a preceding chapter, shown that God pervades the whole universe of matter and mind. By him all things, great and small, animate and inanimate, consist. "Every object in nature is impressed with his foot-print, and each new day repeats the wonders of creation; yes, there is not a morning we open our eyes but they meet a scene as wonderful as that which fixed the gaze of Adam, when he awoke into existence. Nor is there any object, be it a pebble or pearl, weed or rose, the flower-spangled sward beneath or the star-spangled sky above, or worm or an angel, a drop of water or a boundless ocean, in which intelligence may not discern, and piety may not adore, the providence of him who assumed our nature that he might save our souls."

> "This earth, with all its dust and tears,
> Is no less his than yonder spheres;
> And rain-drops weak, and grains of sand,
> Are stamped by his immediate hand."

In discussing the doctrine of a universal providence, we will necessarily pass over some of the same ground we occupied in the preceding chapter. In that chapter we sought to demonstrate that the providence of God was not special, as held by some, nor general, as taught by others, but that one act or operation was just as special as another, and that all the operations of divine providence are in harmony with established laws, or performed by second causes, except when and where a miracle was necessary in order to establish the truth of revealed religion. In this chapter it will be our object to demonstrate that in the kingdom of nature, as well as in the kingdom of grace, the workings of divine providence include not only stupendous matters and events. but also that which seems to be of little or no importance.

The doctrine of a universal providence, like many other sacred doctrines, has often been misunderstood and misapplied. And whilst it may seem to be rather a grave charge to bring against the church of Christ, we think we are not exaggerating when we say that the vast majority of Christians practically limit the operations of divine providence. They profess to believe in a universal providence, but practically deny it. We would not envy the consolation of those who can see the hand of God in the storm and not in the calm, for he is as much in the gentle zephyr that fans the fevered brow, as in the rushing tornado that lays the forest waste. He is as much in the tiny dew-drop that clings to the delicately penciled flower as in the boundless ocean. There is in the belief of a universal, everworking, all-wise, and benevolent providence an exhaustless source of consolation. When delivered from some great danger we say, and properly, too, that God brought us rescue. But we shall see hereafter that we have been delivered from ten thousand dangers by us unseen. Yes, we shall see, as we can not now see, how much our Father in heaven has done for us; and also how wise and benevolent his plans and operations were.

It is cold and cheerless comfort to say to those that are unavoidably poor and afflicted, that they have been overlooked and forgotten. "It is indeed a mockery to the person exposed to heavy affliction, to tell him that God regulates all matters of moment, but has thought it unnecessary to make provision for his particular case." "Thou, God, seest me," was the exclamation of one who was deeply sensible of the omnipresence of God— "seest me," not my neighbor, or my friend, or the world generally, but "me." My thoughts, plans, motives, are all open to the eye of God. Wherever I am, whatever may be my surroundings, my afflictions, temptations, heart-aches, bereavements, dangers, and disappointments, God sees and knows it all. Am I weak, ignorant, faint-hearted? God knows it. And how comforting it is to know and feel that the Supreme Ruler of all things is as merciful and kind, as he is wise and powerful. Beloved, remember that

> "God has marked each sorrowing day,
> And numbered every secret tear,
> And heaven's long years of bliss shall pay,
> For all his children suffer here."

Melancthon said that men are wont to think of God as of a ship-builder, who when he has completed his work, and launched his vessel, leaves it. This was the notion of the Stoics and Epicureans. But revealed religion teaches a purer and better doctrine; it teaches that God not only created all things, but continues with his works from first to last, *for by him all things consist.* The old divines used to speak of providence as a continued creation. The proud atheist may talk and write fluently about the established laws by which the world of matter and mind is controlled; but these are nothing more than God's chosen instrumentalities, by and through which he operates. "Every existence, and every property and quality and act of each is maintained simply by the everlasting power of God. Were this power to be withheld, they would not only cease to have such qualities, but would cease to be."

We have said that the doctrine of a universal providence rests mainly on the fact that God is everywhere present, and would cease to be God if that presence were withdrawn from any part of his creation. He is everywhere not only to uphold, but to govern. Some, perhaps, would regard the world of matter and mind as a machine, which was wound up in the beginning and left to run without further care or concern. Men are constantly more or less inclined to measure the Almighty by themselves, as if he were altogether such a one as they are. How God is everywhere, sustaining and managing all things, and how and why he does this and that, we may not be able to comprehend. We know indeed that all things, material and immaterial, were made by him and for him, and without him was not anything made that was made; and herein is no less of power, wisdom, and goodness, than in upholding and controlling all things.

If the providence of God is not universal, if it does not include every possible or conceivable circumstance in which either men or angels can be placed, it would be exceedingly difficult to understand, much less to draw comfort from passages like this: "Casting all your care upon him, for he careth for you." "All your care," small as well as great, for "all care" necessarily includes the most trifling affairs of life. If it were true that God only concerns himself about such matters as appear to us of greatest moment, there could not be any possible advantage in attempting to cast all care upon him. But when we remember that life in the most insignificant bird is sustained by him, and that we are accounted of far greater value than many sparrows, we are encouraged to draw nigh, and cast all our care upon him, especially since he has given us the blessed assurance that he careth for us.

Christians often fall into trouble on account of their disposition to banish God from what they are pleased to call little things, forgetting that great results are often reached by what seemed to be the most trifling incidents. We see no immediate connection between the infant Moses lying in the ark of rushes, and the man standing on the shore of the Red Sea, with his rod stretched out over the waters, and commanding hundreds of thousands of men, women, and children to stand still and see the salvation of God. But there is a connection, a complete chain composed of many links. When we see the waters rolling up into heaps, and Moses and his company passing safely between them, we say that God was there;

and so he was. But he was as certainly and closely connected with Moses in the ark of rushes as he was when he stood on the bank of the Red Sea. Every link in this wonderful chain was formed under the immediate supervision of the Almighty. "We make too much of our distinctions of greater and smaller, when we carry them into eternity; such quantities reach not Jehovah. It costs him no more thought, no more labor, no more exertion, to maintain an atom in its sunbeam, than to whirl systems of suns, and planets, and satellites along the shining galaxy."

Whoever will take the pains to read and study the history of the world in general, and of the church in particular, will see that it is all illuminated by a light, and animated by a spirit, strangely in contrast with anything we see in matter alone. He will see a shaping and turning of events wholly unaccounted for, without admitting the superintendence of a wisdom, power, and foresight far above and beyond what we find in man. "The philosophy of history can be learned only in the laboratory of heaven, with the eye fixed on the hand that moves the world."

Let me appeal to your life-experience as Christians. Retrace your steps. Go back over your history carefully. Study the numerous events of your own life, with your mind fixed on the various agencies employed in carrying forward the designs of providence. Call up if you can the bright dreams of your youth. How many of these have ripened into realities? Which of you have traveled the road through life you intended to travel? Here at this nook, and there at that corner, an unforeseen circumstance changed your whole course in life. It was no great affair; nothing which at the time seemed to be important. In a word, it was a very little thing; and yet it changed your whole course in life. Who in thus reviewing his life can not see, yes, and feel, the force of the language of Solomon: "A man's heart deviseth his way, but the Lord directeth his steps." You have laid many plans, devised many ways, had many bright dreams, yet not one of them has ever been realized. There was no great event, no shaking of mountains or falling of empires, to change your course; a very little thing did it—a simple thought, a word or look, that was all; but God was there.

Minute events are sometimes made the hinges upon which the most important results turn. Practical chemists inform us that one grain of iodine will impart color to seven thousand times its weight of water. So in life, one thought, one look, one companion, one suggestion, may affect the whole of life. A great ship was to be launched in an English dock-yard. Thousands of persons gathered to see it glide down into the water. All was in readiness: the blocks were removed, but the vessel did not move. The assembly were disappointed. But a little boy ran forward and pushed with all his power. The multitude laughed; but the massive hull started, and away it went into the water. The vessel was almost ready to move, and only needed the few pounds the boy could add to put it in motion. So in life, the most stupendous results often hinge upon the most insignificant causes. "The art of printing, probaby the parent of more good than all others, owes its origin to rude impressions taken for the amusement of children, from letters carved on the bark of a beech-tree. This was a slight matter, which thousands would have passed over with neglect;" but God was in it, and from so slight a beginning such stupendous results have followed.

We are not permitted to see the end from the beginning. We have occasional glimpses of his plans and purposes. But from what little we are permitted to see and understand, we are encouraged to believe that the hand of God is always near; that not one of our individual interests is overlooked or forgotten. In the midst of our reflections upon the wisdom, power, benevolence, and goodness of God, how he formed systems and suns and sustains and whirls them along in their courses, we hear a whisper from the eternal throne: "Fear not little flock; it is your Father's good pleasure to give you the kingdom." Even "the very hairs of your head are all numbered." But "how preposterous," says the skeptic, "to think that God will vary from the line of his sublime acts to meet the case of a poor woman or an insignificant child." "True enough; but God does not vary, he does not deviate. That emergency, that distress, that cry, that deliverance, all are parts of the plan. links of the chain, and this is precisely what we mean by providence."

Afflictions, disappointments, losses, and crosses, are all God's instruments by which problems are solved; some in one way, and some in another. "When we appear in heaven," says an excellent writer, "we shall have to thank God that he so often protected us from ourselves, thwarted our purposes, crossed our passions, blighted our dreams, and blasted the tree we almost made an idol, and of which we prophesied, in our sunny hours, that we would sit down in old age under its shadow, and eat of its pleasant fruits. God put a worm in the gourd; we wept when it withered, but we shall praise him in heaven that it faded and fell, for it was the finger of our God teaching and training his child for a higher destiny and the enjoyment of sweeter fruit."

"There's a divinity that shapes our ends,
Rough hew them how we will."

It will assist us in our conception of the doctrine of a universal providence to remember that its workings are always going forward. Whether we are waking or sleeping, sick or well, living or dying, here or there, providence is ever working. It has no night, no sabbath, no day of rest. God is everywhere, and everywhere at work. He is in the storm, directing the course of the lightning; in the earthquake, controlling its influence; superintending the rolling of the ocean's waves, sustaining the sun, moon, and stars in their courses; watching the comet, with its fiery train, as it rushes through the heavens; observing the forming of every flower, leaf, and spire of grass; feeding the nations of the earth, and attending to the cry of the raven. O blessed thought, how it should warm the heart and quicken the affections of the good man,—I am not overlooked, not forgotten, not left alone. "thou, God, seest me." Christian, you are not asked to prepare your own steps, only to trust in God. The way is all new to you and full of snares and pitfalls: God will lead you, for "as the mountains are round about Jerusalem, so the Lord is round about his people from henceforth even forever." Hark! it is the voice of your Father: "Fear thou not; for I am with thee: be not dismayed; for I am thy God: I will strengthen thee; yea, I will uphold thee with the right hand of my righteousness."

But we are so accustomed to look after God, expecting only to see his majesty and glory displayed in great and terrible events, that we often overlook his presence in the common walks of life. God was evidently in the cloudy, fiery pillar that led Israel through the Red Sea. He was with Moses on the smoking, quaking mountain. We see him in the motions of Arcturus and Pleiades, and his presence is in all the grand operations of nature; but he is as certainly in the gentle dew that refreshes the delicate flower, that blooms and fades unseen in the wilderness, and also nourishes the "tiniest seed-cell of the tiniest moss." "His presence is as real in every atom of dust as in every orb of the skies."

What if we can not see the exact shape of our Father's hand, as he forms the numerous links in the chain of his providence. Can we not afford to trust him of whom it is said that "he hath done all things well?" "Who is among you," asks the prophet, "that feareth the Lord, that obeyeth the voice of his servant, that walketh in darkness, and have no light? let him trust in the name of the Lord, and stay upon his God." There is not a link in the chain that has gone there by accident or chance; not a single turn in the wheel without his permission or direction; and what often seems to us dark and mysterious is only designed for our highest good. God will see to it that nothing can befall his beloved who trust in him, that shall not work out for them a far more exceeding and eternal weight of glory.

> "Yon cottager, who weaves at her own door,
> Pillows and bobbins all her little store,
> Content though mean, and cheerful if not gay,
> Shuffling her threads about the live-long day,
> Just earns a scanty pittance, and at night
> Lies down secure, her heart and pocket light;
> She for her humble sphere by nature fit,
> Has little understanding, and no wit;
> Receives no praise, but though her lot be such
> 'Toilsome and indigent,' she renders much;
> Just knows, and knows no more, her Bible true,—
> A truth the brilliant Frenchmen never knew,
> And in that charter reads with sparkling eyes
> Her title to a treasure in the skies
> O happy peasant! O unhappy lord!
> His the mere tinsel, hers the rich reward;
> He praised, perhaps, for ages yet to come,
> She never heard of half a mile from home;
> He lost in errors his vain heart prefers,
> She safe in the simplicity of hers."

As we before said, the preservation of human life is justly ascribed to God. All who believe the Bible to be the word of God must believe this. But all do not so clearly comprehend that God preserves life by second causes; they accept the whole, but reject the several parts which make up the whole. The preservation of human life, while it is all of God, is not the result of one continued miracle. There must be bread to eat, and water to drink; but the bread is not produced by miracle. The sun must shine and the rain must fall. If these were withheld it would require a constant miracle to perpetuate human existence. The shining of the sun, heat, and rain are all ascribed to God. It is his sun that shines and his rain that falls. This serves to demonstrate the truth of our proposition, that God's providence includes not only the preservation of human life, but all the means employed in its accomplishment, or, in other words, that the providence of God is universal.

The operations of divine providence are as clearly and distinctly manifest in the kingdom of grace as they are, or ever have been, in the kingdom of nature. God is sufficiently wise to devise all the necessary means, and sufficiently powerful to execute all his plans, so that all the interests of his spiritual kingdom shall be preserved and kept out of the hands of the destroyer. The church is to God as the apple of his eye, and when he said, "fear not little flock," he intended to teach them that as a shepherd looked after all his flock, so his care would be extended to each member of his spiritual flock.

The means and instrumentalities employed in sustaining and defending his church are so numerous that only a few of them can be considered in this connection. We shall see in this however as we have seen in his management in the kingdom of nature, that there is a designed correspondence of one event to another; that the chain is perfect and complete in all its parts. And what at the time of their occurrence seemed to be of little or no consequence, was so linked into other events as to produce the most astonishing results. Even such events as seemed to be contingent or accidental, and, to all human appearance, completely detached from everything else, were so controlled and overruled by infinite wisdom and goodness as to fill a vacancy which must otherwise have remained a blank. What, for example, can seem more accidental than a *lot;* but even this is controlled by infinite wisdom. Solomon says, "The lot is cast into the lap; but the whole disposing thereof is of the Lord." Prov. xvi. 33. "Great events often turn upon a very small pivot. A sudden thought in a man's heart, a single sentence from a man's lips, may lead to immense good or incalculable evil, as the history of the world abundantly shows."

A decree went out from Cæsar Augustus that the whole world should be taxed. Now there was nothing remarkable in this. I doubt if either Cæsar or his cabinet saw anything more in it than a national necessity. Neither he nor his advisers intended directly or indirectly to assist in any way in fulfilling a prophecy that had been made hundreds of years before. It may be that they did not know that any such phophecy existed. But under this decree it was necessary that Joseph and Mary should go to their own village to pay the required tribute; and by this was fulfilled the prophecy which said: "Thou, Bethlehem Ephratah, though thou be little among the thousands of Judah, yet out of thee shall he come forth unto me that is to be ruler in Israel; whose goings forth have been from of old, from everlasting." Micah v. 2. Micah was moved by the Holy Ghost to utter this prophecy, and God provided the necessary means, and controlled events so that it was literally fulfilled.

Paul said, "I appeal to Cæsar." There was not anything extraordinary in this. The same thing had been done before. Perhaps Paul himself had no purpose other than to obtain simple justice, which he saw could not be had where he then was. He had been preaching in Judea and Jerusalem for a while, and it would seem that the infant church was but ill-prepared to spare such an accomplished workman. But the appeal had been made, and to Cæsar he must go. According to all human probabilities, if he would go to Rome he would be thrust into some dark dungeon, and so end his ministerial career. But Paul went to Rome; and what might have been considered a blunder in the first place, was so overruled and controlled that it brought about the most stupendous results. "Rome was the very metropolis of the earth,—a word spoken there was like a sound uttered in a whispering gallery; it was repeated and re-echoed to the uttermost bounds of the Roman empire; Christianity, therefore, appearing in Rome, would be sure to be heard of and talked about throughout the whole length and breadth of the civilized world."

Thirty years after Peter had delivered the opening address of the gospel age, Tacitus, the accomplished Latin historian, says of Christianity: "This dire superstition was checked for a while, but it again burst, and not only spread over Judea, the first seat of mischief, but even introduced itself into Rome. The confessions of those who were seized discovered vast multitudes of accomplices. They were convicted of hatred to the human race." Pliny, another Roman writer, says: "The number of Christians is so great as to call for serious consultation. The contagion of this superstition has spread, not only through cities, but through all the villages of the country."

Paul's appeal to Cæsar, although nothing extraordinary in the first place, was made a most powerful means in the hands of an all-wise and ever-working Providence in the early and rapid spread of Christianity among the nations of the earth. In the year 106, Justin Martyr said: "There is not a nation, Greek or barbarian, even those who wander in tribes and live in tents, amongst whom prayers and thanksgivings are not offered to the Father, in the name of Jesus crucified." Is this rapid spread of Christianity to be accounted for by simply saying that everything was in its favor, that the nations of the earth were in waiting for something of that nature? or was it accomplished by the eloquence and superior wisdom of the few illiterate fishermen that had the matter in hand? The truth is, Christianity was met by every conceivable form of opposition; by the sword and faggot, by prisons and banishments, and by the ingenuity and skill of the wise; but in the face of all opposition it went on.

Mr. Gibbon, an infidel writer, unwilling of course to admit the divinity of the religion of Jesus, undertook to account for the early and rapid spread of Christianity by what seemed to him to be satisfactory. The first reason he assigns was the "inflexible zeal of the early Christians." This admission, coming from an enemy, speaks well for the early friends of Jesus. But I am sure, if history is not all a base forgery, the Jews exhibited as much zeal and determination in suppressing it as the apostles did in spreading it. "They were not wanting in zeal when they kindle ' the martyrs' fires, and made such efforts to put it down."

Another reason assigned by Gibbon, was "the more complete manifestation of a future state." This is another good admission; but it is of no possible advantage to Mr. Gibbon's side of the question, for both the Jews and pagans believed not only in a future state, but in future rewards and punishments. Paul, in defending himself against Tertullus (Acts xxiv. 15), declares that "they themselves also allow, that there shall be a resurrection of the dead, both of the just and unjust." He held nothing by which their general creed might be altered in reference to the present or future state,—nothing but what they themselves allowed.

Another reason he assigns was "the miraculous powers ascribed to the primitive Christians." Now suppose all these were impostures, huge pretensions, it certainly does not speak well for the learning and intelligence of Rome to say that none of them were able to detect and expose the deception. Mr. Gibbon assigns other reasons very similar to those we have given, not one of which is any more plausible than the foregoing. The only rational conclusion is, that God governed, controlled, and overruled all the events and incidents, great and small, in such a way as to secure the designed results. The history of Moses, Daniel, Stephen, John, together with the history of the introduction and spread of Christianity in the Roman empire, Abyssinia, Iberia, Britain, Bulgaria, and our own land, demonstrates that the hand of God was in the movement from first to last, and that more than once the wrath of man was made to praise God.

Christians, learn from this that "in all circumstances Christianity is safe. All the popes of Rome can not extinguish the Bible; all the grand dukes of Tuscany can not imprison Christianity. Religion dies not with its martyrs; Christianity departs not with its professors. Pyramids shall be reduced to ruin, and the great granite hills from which they were dug shall be scattered like dust before the wind; but Christianity has God for its author, omnipotence for its shield, and eternity for its glorious life; and when this dispensation shall have passed away, it will only have given place to a better. The olive and the palm shall grow upon the soil that is beaten hard by the soldiers' feet; the ramparts of cities shall become the gardens of the citizens." Fear thou not; the little stone that came out of the mountain will yet fill the whole earth. The wilderness shall blossom as the rose, and streams break out in desert places. Christianity shall live until

> "The lambs with wolves shall graze the verdant mead,
> And boys in flowery lands the tiger lead.
> The steer and lion in one crib shall meet,
> And harmless serpents lick the pilgrim's feet.
> The smiling infant in his hand shall take
> The crested basilisk and speckled snake;
> Pleased, the green luster of the scales survey,
> And with their forked tongues shall innocently play."

But let us descend in the history of the Christian church, and note a few events. Some of these may be mysterious, but by careful study it may be seen that the hand of God was working all the time. For purposes not so readily comprehended by us, God permitted a night of a thousand years to gather around the church. All along through this night, error grew and spread with astonishing rapidity, until the spiritual worship of God was well-nigh lost in ignorance and superstition. Toward the close of this long night, a man was born in Eisleben. So poor and destitute was he that he went out on the streets, when yet but a small lad, to play the flute from door to door, that he might thereby procure his daily bread. Accidentally, as we are wont to say, the wife of one Conrad Cotta saw his distress and took him in and gave him bread. She became interested in the boy, and presently succeeded in enlisting the sympathies of other ladies, and he was sent to college. *Accidentally* he found a Bible, read it, and obtained spiritual light. But who is Martin Luther? A poor penniless boy, wandering about the streets in Eisenach, without any aim other than to gain a morsel of bread. And yet, in a few years this unpretending youth, by his eloquence and power in the pulpit, is to startle and illuminate all Europe and America. Now in all this we do not see the ingenuity and cunning craftiness of men, but the "finger of God."

"Let us notice," says an excellent writer, "what unprovoked attempts were made to quench the light that the reformers had kindled, and to arrest the progress of that faith, the blessings and privileges of which we now enjoy. Philip the Second, personated by the Duke of Alva, kindled those terrible wars in the Low Countries, that resulted in the Protestantism of Holland. The same monarch arranged the Invincible Armada. It was consecrated by the reigning pope; and in order that England might offer no obstructions to the progress of this fleet, filled as it was with instruments of torture and death for the heretics, the pope deposed Queen Elizabeth, and released all her subjects from any duty or allegiance that they owed to her, and then sent the armada, blessed and consecrated by himself, to our shores. But God saw this whole movement from the beginning to the end, as well as the motives that prompted it. The admiral of the fleet died upon the voyage; many of the ships were buried in the deep, and finally the whole fleet was completely destroyed. Then Queen Elizabeth, with that piety which ought never to be forgotten, had medals struck commemorating the deliverance of her country, with these words engraved on them: '*Afflaret Deuset dissipantur,*'—'God breathed upon the armada, and it was scattered to the winds,' or she might have said, this is the Lord's doings, and it is marvelous in our eyes."

The Rev. Mr. Charles, while preaching in Wales, found in his pastoral work a number of families that were destitute of the Bible. He considered how it might be possible to meet this great want. It was but a single thought in the beginning, yet this little incident brought into subsequent operation the British and Foreign Bible Society. Look now at the results of that one thought. Millions of copies of the Holy Scriptures have been scattered through the world, and the poorest of the poor may sit by his own dim fire and read of the way that leads to that far-away home where all may be kings and priests unto God and the Lamb forever. As the heaven is high above the earth, so the ways and purposes of the Almighty are above the ways and purposes of man.

Mr. Robert Raikes saw a number of children on the street, neglected. A single thought was suggested to his mind: "Can anything be done for them?" This thought expanded and begat other thoughts, and when communicated to other minds produced similar feelings of interest. And thus step by step the interest grew, until the little rill became a river. And now in Europe and America, and on the islands of the sea, the blessed Sunday-school work is going on, by which multiplied thousands of children are instructed out of the word of life. With our hearts and minds fixed on God's providential workings in sustaining and advancing the interests of his spiritual kingdom among men, we can not fail to feel an interest in the language of the sweet singer of Israel, when he said: "I will meditate on all thy works; I muse on the work of thy hand." "Come and see the work of God." "Oh that men would praise the Lord for his wonderful works to the children of men. The works of the Lord are great; sought out of all them that have pleasure in them."

In tracing the history of the church, from the time it was made public in the family of Abraham, down to this period, we can find innumerable instances in which the hand of God was directly concerned. We can see in such review how he has been with his people, opening a door for success here and thwarting the designs of an enemy there, often bringing the most stupendous results out of small beginnings; how he has turned and overturned the works and designs of men; how one link of this mysterious chain was joined to another, not by the wisdom of even good men, but by an ever-working, all-wise, and glorious providence.

God has been and still is with the church, turning to her advantage a thousand instrumentalities and agencies. And at times when the most pious men trembled for the safety of the church, God was preparing means to bring his people out of the wilderness. While Secker was deploring the "demoralization of England," and Burnet saw "imminent danger hanging over the church," and Watts was writing that "religion was dying out in the world;" when in fact the whole church had become "an ecclesiastical system, under which the people of England had lapsed into heathenism, and the French philosophers were spreading contagion through Europe. God was preparing the means, apparently disconnected but providentially coincident, which were to resuscitate the the dying faith, and introduce the era of modern evangelization in the Protestant world." If we could but see, there is a chain of events, coincident, running far into the past and reaching far into the future, that would lead us out of many doubts and fears. We would see how for a long while the lines of history converged toward Calvary, and now how they diverge from Calvary, running backward and forward in every conceivable direction from one common center, and pointing to one common end, and how, in spite of the devices of men and devils, the Son of God will continue to reign until the kingdoms of this world shall become the kingdoms of our Lord, "for he must reign, until he hath put all enemies under his feet."

> "Rise, crowned with light, imperial Salem, rise!
> Exalt thy towering head, and lift thine eyes!
> See a long race thy spacious courts adorn;
> See future sons and daughters yet unborn,
> In crowding ranks on every side arise,
> Discarding life, impatient for the skies!
> See barbarous nations at thy gates attend,
> Walk in thy light, and in thy temple bend."

CHAPTER VII.

PROVIDENCE OVERRULETH ALL THINGS. GOOD AND EVIL ARE CONTROLLED BY HIM.

"All nature is but art, unknown to thee;
All chance, direction which thou canst not see;
All discord, harmony not understood."

The great majority of the human race, in all time past, whether pagan or Christian, have agreed that it was glorious to create a universe like ours; but the majority do not clearly comprehend that it is equally glorious to manage and control it. All agree that God, or the gods, created all things, and governs in a sort of general way, but can not perceive that this control extends to evil things as well as good, or that it can include everything without detracting from the dignity of the Creator. The proposition we propose to discuss in this chapter we will state thus: *All things, great and small, good and evil, are under the control of the Almighty, and can not exist without his permission.*

We know, indeed, that herein there is a mystery. How an evil act may be foreseen, predicted, and provided against, while at the same time the actors in the foreseen evil are left perfectly free and perfectly accountable, we may not be able to comprehend. There is no conflict between the sovereignty of God and man's responsibility, no matter how mysterious and intricate it may appear to our minds. In the preceding chapters we demonstrated, from the plainest possible declarations of the Holy Scriptures, that God governs all things, and that the very idea of providence includes foresight and provision. There is, however, a vast difference between foreseeing an event and providing for it, and predetermining that the event should occur. It was predicted that Jerusalem should be destroyed. Now did this prediction produce that event? God foresaw that it would come to pass; hence the event produced the prophecy, but not the prophecy the event.

In foreseeing that a particular crime would be committed, and then bringing into existence the very persons that God foresaw would commit that crime, is considered by some divines as equivalent to predetermining that the crime should be committed by those persons, and that they had no power to do otherwise. But in foreseeing the crime and the persons that would commit that crime, he also foresaw the use that the person or persons would make of their moral agency; and the fact that he foresaw how they would use their agency, did not directly or indirectly affect their power to do evil or good. We see acts which are past, while he sees all acts, whether past, present, or yet to come. "Known unto God are all his works from the beginning." Everything is present with the Almighty. We use the term *foreseen* because it is in common use, and we know what meaning to attach to it. A crime was committed yesterday, and we know it to-day, with all the circumstances connected with it; but our knowing it to-day had no possible influence over the parties that were connected with the affair. All things are known to God as though they were past,—he sees the end from the beginning. God predetermined that all men should be free agents, and at the same time saw the exact use they would make of that power, and the result. He did not predetermine the act, he only foresaw it. It was prophesied that Babylon should fall. God saw this, with all the circumstances that would lead to it, and moved the heart of the prophet to utter the prediction. But the persons that operated in the accumulation of the crimes that brought upon them this destruction, were as free to act and as fully responsible for their acts as though God had not foreseen it.

Dr. Clarke, in order to explain the apparent difficulty arising from a belief in the foreknowledge of God, allows that it was possible for him to determine not to know. But this view, instead of relieving, only increases the difficulty. It would be as hard for us to understand how it were possible for God to determine not to know a thing before he knew it, as to comprehend how he could foresee an act and yet not predetermine it. Then, also, it would involve another difficulty, for if God would determine not to know, then he would determine not to be omniscient, and when he would cease to be omniscient, he would cease to be God

But it was not our purpose to discuss at length the question of foreknowledge, only so far as it might be necessary to prepare the mind for a proper contemplation of an overruling power. We pass to consider that God, in the order of his divine providence, overrules and controls the acts and designs of men, whether they be good or evil, in such a manner that in the end his glory is promoted. How one event is connected with another, and how long the train of events may be by which an evil act or design is overruled, we may not be permitted to know. A single act in a man's life to-day may be a link in the almost endless chain of events, by which an evil act or design a thousand years hence is to be overruled. We are to-day enjoying the blessing of a pure Christianity; but we do not see any immediate connection between this and Martin Luther playing his flute in the streets in Eisenach in order to get his daily bread. Nevertheless, there is a connection. So in overruling evil designs, the work of preparation may occupy a long time; but in all the events coincident with each other the free will of man is never interfered with. To assume that evil designs and acts are not foreseen, controlled, and overruled is to assume that the Bible is not true.

No other of the sacred writers had clearer conceptions of the sovereignty of God than David. His declaration is this: "Surely the wrath of man shall praise thee: the remainder of wrath shalt thou restrain." Ps. lxxvi. 10. The rage of man, however criminal in itself, shall only serve to manifest in some way or other the glory of God. Solomon says: "There are many devices in a man's heart; nevertheless the counsel of the Lord, that shall stand." Prov. xix. 21. Again he says that "a man's heart deviseth his way: but the Lord directeth his steps." Prov. xvi. 9. Man proposes, but God disposes. He deviseth in his heart to do evil, and may do it, but God overrules it, so that good results from it.

"All is best, though we oft doubt
What the unsearchable depose
Of highest wisdom brings about,
And ever best found in the close."

The case of Daniel will seem to illustrate the truth of our proposition. He was a good man, and, like many other good men, had his enemies. These enemies sought to destroy him. God permitted them to do their worst, but all the while saw the result, and so controlled the incidents that the end was reached. Those wicked men prevailed upon the king to issue a decree by which all persons in his dominion were forbidden to pray to the living God. Now, when Daniel knew that the decree had been signed by which it became a law, he went to his chamber and prayed as aforetime. This was precisely what his enemies had expected, and when they saw it they immediately reported it to the king. The penalty attached to this decree was that the violator should be cast into a den of lions. Daniel was found guilty, and was thrown in among the lions. Thus far these wicked men were permitted to have their own way. They had no other purpose than to get Daniel out of the way. But in this the wrath of man was made to praise God; for instead of accomplishing their wicked intentions they brought upon themselves sudden and terrible disaster. There is a very great contrast between the first and second decree of King Darius. The one was issued before Daniel was cast into the den of lions, and the other afterward. As illustrating forcibly how God can overrule the designs and purposes of men, we will insert both decrees. "Whosoever shall ask a petition of any God or man for thirty days, save of thee, O king, he shall be cast into the den of lions." Dan. vi. 7. This decree was signed, proclaimed, and executed. Subsequently Darius issued another decree, which ran thus: " I make a decree, That in every dominion of my kingdom men tremble and fear before the God of Daniel: for he is the living God, and steadfast for ever, and his kingdom that which shall not be destroyed, and his dominion shall be even unto the end. He delivereth and rescueth, and he worketh signs and wonders in heaven and in earth, who hath delivered Daniel from the power of the lions." Dan. vi. 26, 27. This looks verily as if the king's heart was in the hand of the Lord. The history of Shadrach, Meshach, and Abed-nego (Dan. iii.) is another equally striking illustration of God's overruling providence,—how he turned and overturned the evil purposes of men to the glory of his own great name.

We see in the life of Joseph a clear and distinct exhibition of the hand of God. His brethren, out of envy and malice, sold him into Egypt. This was a wicked act, prompted by an evil design, and the parties were just as guilty before God and man as they would have been if nothing but the worst of evils had resulted from it. But this was all foreseen and provided for. Joseph recognized the hand of God in the whole affair; for after he was made known to his brethren, he said to them: "As for you, ye thought evil against me, but God meant it for good, to bring to pass, as it is to-day, to save much people alive." "Ye thought evil." Your intention was all wrong. But see how quickly he turned it. "But God meant it for good." God permitted it to be so, and then overruled it for good. The overruling providence of God was so clearly manifest, that Joseph speaks of it in such pointed language, the meaning of which we can not mistake. "God sent me," he declares, "before you. It was not you that sent me hither, but God." You had no such intention; you intended evil, and only evil, but God meant it for good, that is, he brought good out of it.

The death of Christ was an evil act on the part of those who accomplished it. Their intention was to murder the son of Mary, and they made use of all the means that would have been necessary to reach that end in the case of any ordinary man. Now in all this every incident had been foreseen, predicted, and provided for in the ages that were past. Four thousand years were occupied in the work of preparation, during which time events were continually transpiring which invariably pointed to the suffering of Christ. Peter speaks of the death of Christ in bold language. "Him, being delivered by the determinate counsel and foreknowledge of God, ye have taken, and by wicked hands have crucified and slain." Acts ii. 23. The "determinate counsel of God" implies that he had in his own infinite mind determined the time, place, and circumstances of his death. He saw what time and place would be most proper. God had determined that the salvation of a lost world should be secured in that way. He had determined from the foundation of the world to give his Son to die for its redemption. Rev. xiii. 8. "And the treachery of Judas and the malice of the Jews were only the incidental means by which the great counsel of God was fulfilled; the counsel of God intending the sacrifice, but never ordering that it should be brought about by such wretched means. This was permitted, the other decreed." God decreed that his Son should come into the world to offer salvation to a lost race. He foresaw how he would be put to death. This he permitted, and the parties were none the less guilty on that account. This is fully implied in the language of Peter when he charges them with the crime. "By wicked hands ye slew him." I will once more state that all the predictions relating to the sufferings and death of the Son of God, with all the incidents connected therewith, were not the result of any predetermination. God predetermined to give his Son, and foresaw the treatment he would receive, and this foreknowledge of events produced the prophecy. But the whole event, with all the incidents connected therewith, and wicked designs of his crucifiers, was so overruled as to produce the highest good of a lost race.

To illustrate the truth of our proposition still farther we will take the case of the Assyrian monarch invading and punishing the Hebrews. "I will send him against a hypocritical nation, and against the people of my wrath will I give him a charge, to take the spoil, and to take the prey, and to tread them down like the mire of the streets. Howbeit he meaneth not so, neither doth his heart think so; but it is in his heart to destroy and cut off nations not a few." Isa. x. 6, 7. The Assyrian committed sin during his invasion, and in this act he was entirely free, although this crime had been foreseen and predicted. but not predetermined; he was free to act, and entirely responsible for the act. But by this act, foreseen but not foredetermined, God in his wonder-working providence so overruled and controlled the circumstances that the very thing intended was accomplished. To show that the Assyrian acted with perfect freedom of will, God denounces the crime, and severely punishes him for it,—which a just and holy being could not and would not have done if it had been predetermined that the crime should be committed. The whole affair, from beginning to end, seems to illustrate this simple truth, that the operations of divine providence include evil acts and designs as well as good acts and good designs.

There would not be any great consolation arising from the belief that God only overrules good acts. However widely his government may differ in regard to good and evil designs, it is nevertheless true that his providence includes all. God permits evil to exist, "but he contemplates free acts as free acts, and in no degree puts forth any causative influences to tempt or compel to the commission of crimes." But in his far-reaching and universal plans, evil deeds are permitted and then overruled. Take the following case: A poor but pious woman, who had been much persecuted by a wicked husband, on returning from the house of God was first abused, and then struck to the floor. The good woman, who had learned not to return evil for evil, rose and said to her husband: "You have struck me on the one cheek, and, as Christ hath commanded me, I turn the other to you. If you have the heart to do it smite that also, and I will cheerfully bear it for his sake who has this night promised to give me strength for my day and trial." The man's heart was struck with a conviction that there was something above nature which enabled his wife to bear such treatment in such a spirit. He afterward accompanied her to the house of God, and soon became a devoted Christian. God foresaw what would occur, and so strengthened the woman's heart that she could bear the abuse. He permitted that wicked man to strike the cruel blow, and then so overruled it that the wrath of man was made to praise him.

Christians are sometimes sorely pressed in spirit under their afflictions, because they can not see a providence in them. They were brought on, perhaps, by some act of their own. "Very well, God can make the wicked acts of men a sword to punish others, and even themselves." God can as well correct us by our own acts as by the acts of others. But "let no man say, when he is tempted, I am tempted of God; for God can not be tempted with evil, neither tempteth he any man." We are free agents. If God chooses to overrule our acts, whether they be good or evil, for our own benefit or the benefit of others, he can do so; but we are not to conclude that because God permits evil, and then overrules it, that he therefore loves it.

God permits sinners to live, but is angry with them every day. He hates sin in every conceivable form. "All the boundless combinations and interchanges of matter and mind, all the play of wheel in wheel, of cause in cause, of thought in thought, of passion in passion, conspire to work out one and the same result—the glory of God." "For of him, and through him, and in him are all things." "Lo, these are parts of his ways; but how little a portion is heard of him? but the thunder of his power who can understand?" Job xxvi. 14.

It is God's chosen method to work by means; but the means are not uniform in their appearance, nor in their effects. Again, opposite effects may be produced by the use of the very same means. "Suppose," says Spencer, "you were in a smith's shop, and there should see several sorts of tools, some crooked, some bowed, others hooked; would you condemn all these things for naught, because they do not look handsome? The smith makes use of them all for the doing of his work. Thus it is with the providences of God; they seem to us to be very crooked and strange, yet they all carry on God's work." Bowers says, "Every bullet has its billet." Beadle says, "All providences to a gracious heart are but so many fulfillments of promises." Charnock says, "All

God's providences are but his touch of the strings of the great instrument of the world." Rutherford says, "The chariot of God's providence runneth not upon broken wheels." Another says, "A crust of God's earning is better than a banquet of our own providing."

<blockquote>
"The bud may have a bitter taste,
But sweet will be the flower.'
</blockquote>

The history of the recent but never to be forgotten rebellion in our own country furnishes us with a remarkable instance of God's overruling providence,—how he can make the wrath and evil designs of men to praise him. Without entering into details, we shall only point out a few incidents to illustrate our proposition. No matter what political party may have been the immediate cause of the war, God suffered it to come, and then controlled and overruled the numerous incidents, so that results widely different from those anticipated were reached.

When the rebellion was first inaugurated, it is not at all probable that any man in the nation comprehended its magnitude. Its course was for the most part strange and inexplicable. Defeats came when least expected. But few men thought that it would result in the destruction of slavery; and even those who were conscientiously opposed to the institution of slavery did not think so.

And on the other side, those who acted the most conspicuous part had no other intention than to make the institution perpetual. But God, who foresaw all that would come to pass, so adjusted and controlled the circumstances that the very thing was accomplished which he determined should be accomplished. No man, whether living or dead, is entitled to any praise for the abolition of slavery, only so far as he acted as an instrument in the hands of God. The slaves are free, and it is all the result of God's wonder-working providence.

The vast majority of those that were opposed to slavery manifested a willingness, at different times during the struggle, to compromise and leave slavery where it was. But all such propositions were set aside. There was a strange and mysterious overruling of events. first a victory on one side then on the other, success and disaster following each other; the nation was terribly tried in the steady furnace-heat of war. Hearts and heads were busily at work to find out the nearest road to peace. Finally it became a necessity—a military necessity—to issue the proclamation of emancipation. But even this was conditional. If those in rebellion would lay down their arms within a hundred days, the institution of slavery would remain. But the proposition was rejected, and the proclamation went into effect. Now, whatever may have been the private sentiments of the chief magistrate of the country and his advisers in reference to the institution of slavery, it is very evident that the proclamation was strictly a war measure. And but for this apparent necessity it would never have been issued. But the hand of God was in it, directing and managing the circumstances in such a manner as to force this necessity upon them, and finally to bring the great problem of emancipation to a complete solution.

For wise purposes the children of Israel were kept wandering in the wilderness of Sinai for forty years. If they had been prepared to enter the promised land, a few days would have been sufficient to have gone from the Red Sea to Jordan. But they were not ready, and hence God kept them in the wilderness until they were ready. So in our struggle, if the people north and south had been willing to let the oppressed go free, the war would have ended long before it did, and thousands of lives would have been spared. But the people were not ready,—neither north nor south,—and hence the struggle continued until the nation was driven by irresistible necessity to let the oppressed go free. God had heard the cries of the downtrodden until the nation's cup was full and poured out. The nation wept under the chastening rod of God, and when they were willing to do right, the angel of peace returned. If slavery was wrong, if its abolition was morally right, the praise of the tardily-given emancipation is due to God, and to him only.

The operations of divine providence are often concealed from our view. Events are occurring which seem to be so perfectly natural that we are often disposed to think that the hand of God has nothing whatever to do with them. The sun shines, the rain falls, the wind blows, all the result of natural causes; hence we say that God had nothing to do with it. But in this we forget that God often, and indeed mostly, operates through natural causes. If God should have sent an angel to free the slaves, then, to be sure, all would have said God did it. But the history of the past furnishes us with these facts. God at sundry times used human agencies to carry forward his plans and accomplish his purposes. Sometimes one nation was employed to scourge another nation; and then again, one part of a nation has been used to scourge another part. Or a man may become his own scourge; and the dealing is just as much under the control of God as if he had sent legions of angels to accomplish it. But we are so anxious to see miracles, some wonderful phenomenon, some upheaving of the works of nature, some wrecking of worlds, that we are not satisfied with the ordinary workings of our Father's hand. But we should see miracles all the time, if our eyes were not closed. On the 5th of August, 1530, there was an awful crisis for the Reformation, when the firmest hearts seemed to swerve, and the boldest trembled. Luther thus wrote to Chancellor Bench: "I have recently witnessed two miracles. This is the first: As I was at my window I saw the stars and the sky, and that vast and glorious firmament in which the Lord has placed them. I could nowhere discover the columns on which the Master has supported his immense vault; and yet the heavens did not fall. And here is the second: I beheld thick clouds hanging above us like a vast sea. I could neither perceive the ground on which they reposed, nor the cords by which they were suspended; and yet they did not fall upon us, but saluted us rapidly, and fled away." So if we could see and comprehend how God is managing the affairs of this world, permitting evil acts and then overturning them to his glory,—how he bringeth the devices of the wicked to naught,—we too would say that we have witnessed miracles.

The enemies of John determined to put him out of the way. They laid hands on him to put him to death, but failing in this, they caused him to be banished to the island of Patmos, supposing, of course, that by separating him from his friends and the church they would cut off his influence. Now God permitted his servant to be treated in this cruel manner, intending to bring good out of it. So on the first day of the week, which was very soon after John had been landed on the island, God appeared unto him, and gave him such a revelation as no man had ever seen before. John's banishment to that dreary island was one link in the chain of events that brought back to the world some of the brightest and most cheering views of the heavenly state. He saw what no man had ever seen. And while his enemies were rejoicing over their fine success in getting him out of the way, he was looking into the very heart of the city of God, and with perfect rapture contemplating the resplendent glory of his final home.

When Paul was a prisoner at Rome he wrote to the church at Philippi on this wise: "I would ye should understand, brethren, that the things which happened unto me have fallen out rather unto the furtherance of the gospel." Phil. i. 12. Those who were instrumental in making Paul a prisoner at Rome had no manner of intention of furthering the gospel of Christ, but directly the reverse. They intended to destroy the life of Paul, and stop the spreading of the gospel. God saw this whole transaction, and understood perfectly their design. He permitted them to do their worst, and then turned their designs upside down, and sent out his gospel in every direction from the city of Rome. The Christian's God is a wonderful God. "A man's heart deviseth his way: but the Lord directeth his steps." Prov. xvi. 9. "There are many devices in a man's heart; nevertheless the counsel of the Lord, that shall stand." Prov. xix. 21.

Such incidents—and if our limits would permit we might furnish many more—assist us in understanding the meaning of the apostle when he said: "All things work together for good to them that love God." Understand, it is only to those who love God that this promise is given. Things often work together for good to wicked persons; but the promise is especially to those that love God. While they work for God, his providences are working for them. He presses everything into his service, so that all things are made to contribute, in some way or other, to the general good of those that love God. We see Balaam starting out with the fixed intention of cursing Israel, but he blesses instead thereof.

There is not a morsel of comfort in that theory which excludes the idea of an overruling providence; that allows all evil acts and designs to have their own way; which declares that God either can not or will not control them. But we know better; God has overruled the evil designs of wicked men, and will do it as often as he please. There is no evil that can befall a true Christian without his permission. Satan had to get permission before he could lay his hand on Job. God is able to do wonderful things in the use of small means, when he chooses to do so. Sometimes he permits his beloved to be handled roughly, that he may thereby convince his enemies of the truth of religion. "A vessel of North Shields sailed from that port, bound for London. The carpenter of the ship alone seemed desirous of private devotion; and, though often ridiculed by his shipmates, continued nevertheless to serve the Lord. In a gale of wind during the voyage, the vessel lay to off Flamborough Head. John, the carpenter, went into the cook-house and kneeled down to implore the blessing of God on the ship and crew. While thus engaged a heavy sea broke over the deck, and hurried him into the foaming sea. One of the crew saw him go overboard, and alarmed the watch by calling out, 'The carpenter overboard.' Consternation seized every mind, and especially when they saw that it was impossible to render him any assistance. The gale increased, and in a moment a back sea dashed across the deck, carried away the stanchions, and left the carpenter on board. When John recovered he found himself on his knees on board his own ship. The crew, seeing this deliverance, cried out with astonishment, 'The carpenter's religion is right; he is favored of God.'" This incident is given in ? little work by the Presbyterian Board of Publication.

Often whilst on the weary journey of life the heart grows faint, and sometimes even sad. Misfortunes seldom come alone. Now a dear friend, a father, mother, brother, sister, husband, wife, or child, is suddenly called away; then losses, disappointments, and afflictions follow in quick succession. We look above and around, and no one seems to care whether our way is rough or smooth. Then with Jacob we are ready to say, "All these things are against me;" and with Rachel, "I am weary of life." Under some such circumstances the psalmist exclaimed, "Oh that I had wings like a dove! for then would I fly away, and be at rest." Child of sorrow and affliction, know thou that "our light affliction, which is but for a moment, worketh for us a far more exceeding and eternal weight of glory." God has not forgotten you. You should not think that because he uses the chastening rod, that he is therefore angry with you. For "whom the Lord loveth he chasteneth, and scourgeth every son whom he receiveth." He may suffer you to be thrown into the furnace, not that you may be destroyed, but purified. The stroke will fall lighter, if we draw nigh to the hand that handles the rod.

> "When urged by strong temptation to the brink
> Of guilt and ruin, stands the virtuous mind,
> With scarce a step between; all-pitying Heaven,
> Severe in mercy, chastening in its love,
> Ofttimes in dark and awful visitation,
> Doth interpose, and leads the wanderer back
> To the straight path, to be forever after
> A firm, undaunted, onward-bearing traveler.
> Strong in humility, who swerves no more."

Friends of Jesus, bear in mind that although for a time wicked men may seem to gain the ascendancy over you, it is only temporary. Your Father in heaven loves you. "Can a mother forget her child?" This would be most unnatural, and seldom if ever occurs. Yet she may; but God says, I will not forget you. To illustrate the strength of a mother's love, I will here record a circumstance. Some years ago, on one of the northern lakes, a vessel was discovered to be on fire. It was some distance from land, and all hope of escape seemed to be cut off. The captain ordered the vessel to be directed toward the nearest point of land. The flames meanwhile continued to spread with fearful rapidity. It soon became apparent that the boat could not be brought to the shore, and the passengers would be compelled to perish in the flames or in the water. Among the passengers on board was a family consisting of a husband, wife, and two children. The husband was a stout man and an excellent swimmer, and so determined to make one terrible effort to save himself and family. By means of a small rope, which happened to be at hand, he tied his wife and children to his body in such a manner as not to interfere with the use of his limbs. Then, after a few words of instruction and encouragement to his wife, he committed himself, with his precious charge, to the water. For a while he struggled manfully; but the burden was heavy, and the waves and wind were against him. He felt that his strength was rapidly failing, and the shore was yet some distance off. At last he said to his wife: "Oh, what shall I do; my strength is almost gone." His wife, heroine as she was, said in reply: "Cut me loose, but save my babes." The husband, nerved by such evidence of love and self-devotion, made another almost superhuman effort. But again his strength and courage were about to fail, and he said to his wife: "My dear, we will perish together." "No," said his wife, "let me perish, but save my babes." Once more he summoned his remaining strength and skill, and succeeded in reaching the shore. Here we have exhibited the strength of a mother's love for her child. Yet God says she may forget; but *I* will not forget those that trust in *me*. God's love to his children is infinitely stronger than the love of a mother to her offspring.

"Eternal love doth keep,
In his complacent arms, the earth, the air, the deep."

"All things that are on earth shall wholly pass away,
Except the love of God, which shall live and last for ay."

CHAPTER VIII.

PROVIDENCE—MYSTERIOUS.

"Each particle of matter is an immensity, each leaf a world, each insect an inexplicable compendium."—*Lavater.* "Sinful man saved in Christ always was, always will be, a mystery, a wonder."—*T. Adams.* "Happy is the man who is content to traverse this ocean to the haven of rest without going into the wretched diving-bells of his own fancies. There are depths; but depths are for God."—*Evans.* "I would fain know all that I need, and all that I may. I leave God's secrets to himself. It is happy for me that God makes me of his court, and not of his council."—*Bishop Hall.* "For my thoughts are not your thoughts, neither are your ways my ways, saith the Lord. For as the heavens are higher than the earth, so are my ways higher than your ways, and my thoughts than your thoughts." Is. lv. 8, 9. "Who is among you that feareth the Lord, that obeyeth the voice of his servant, that walketh in darkness, and hath no light? let him trust in the name of the Lord, and stay upon his God."

Is. 1. 10. "For now we see through a glass darkly." I. Cor. xiii. 11. "It is the glory of God to conceal a thing." Prov. xxv. 2. "He hath made everything beautiful in his time: also he hath set the world in their heart, so that no man can find out the work that God maketh from the beginning to the end." Eccl. iii. 11.

God governs and controls the affairs of this world after the counsel of his own will. Mysteries there are, deep and inexplicable mysteries in God's dealings with the children of men. It seldom, if ever, appears to any man that all things are working together for his good. There are crosses and losses, afflictions and disappointments, about which the very best of men have been tried. There are strange, uneven paths into which good men are sometimes forced, for which at the time they can see no reason. What God has written even a fool may learn to read, but a wise man can not read what God has not written. For

"God moves in a mysterious way,
　His wonders to perform;
　He plants his footsteps in the sea,
　And rides upon the storm."

Dr. McCosh has most beautifully, and I think very aptly, illustrated the inexplicability of divine providence. And lest I should mar the illustration I will give it entire. He says, "The events of providence appear very much like the letters thrown into a post-bag, and then sent forth on their destination. The person who carries them,

> 'Messenger of joy,
> Perhaps to thousands, and of grief to some;
> To him indifferent whether grief or joy.'

Onward he moves, quite unconcerned as to the nature of the communications he bears, or the effect produced by them. And when he looks into the repository it may seem as if its contents were an inextricable confusion, and we wonder how the letters, parcels, money, periodicals, should ever reach their individual destination. But then every letter has its special address inscribed upon it,—it has the name and residence of the party, and so it shall in due time fall into his hands, and bring its proper intelligence. And what different purposes do these letters fulfill—what varied emotions do they excite! This declares that friends are in health and prospering; this other is the bearer of the news of wealth, of the wealth itself; this third tells of some crushing disappointment, and quenches long-cherished hopes by the tidings of the utter failure of deep-planned schemes; while this fourth, with sable symbols, announces to the wife that she is a widow, or to the parent that he is childless, or to the child fondly cherished by the mother that he is an orphan. It is a kind of picture of the movements of providence. What a crowd of events huddled together, and apparently confused, does it carry along with it! Very diverse are the objects bound up in that bundle; very varied are the emotions which they are to excite when opened up. Yet how coolly and systematically does the vehicle proceed on its way. Neither the joy nor the sorrow which it produces causes it to linger an instant in its course. But meanwhile every occurrence, or bundle of occurrences, is let out at its proper place. Each has a name inscribed upon it; each has a place to which it is addressed. Each too has a message to carry, and a purpose to fulfill. Some inspire hope or joy, others raise only fear and sorrow. The events which are unfolded by the same course of things, and which fall out the same day, bring gladness to one and land another in deepest distress. On the occurrence of the same events you perceive one weeping and another rejoicing. Some of the dispensations are destined to propagate prosperity through a whole community. And those others, so black and dismal, and of which so many arrive at the same time, carry, as they are scattered, gloom into the abodes of thousands. But amid all this seeming confusion every separate event has its separate destination. If pestilence has only some one person devoted to it in a city or community, that person it will assuredly find out, and execute the judgment of Heaven upon him. If there be a thousand persons allotted to it in a district, it will not allow one of the thousand to escape. If among the number who are dying there be one regarding whom it has no commission to seize upon him, that individual must remain untouched. 'A thousand shall fall at thy side, and ten thousand at thy right hand, but it shall not come nigh thee.' It has a commission and will execute it; but then it can not go beyond its commission. And in regard to every person to whom the events come, it has a special end to accomplish; and it bears a special message, if he will but read it and attend to it."

Beloved, there is a message in the post-bag for you, and it is being rapidly conveyed along. Whether it be a message of sorrow or of joy, none can tell. If it be of sorrow, the post will not linger; if it be of joy, he will not hasten. It may arrive to-day or perhaps to-morrow. Of the contents of this message you know nothing. The future is all wrapped in impenetrable mystery. We can not tell where our next step will fall. It may be in death's cold waters, in sickness, in adversity, or it may be prosperity. We are advancing. The distance between us and the grave is continually growing less. The chances for life are rapidly narrowing down. Some are now brushing the dew from Jordan's banks. The living know that they must die; but of the trials, afflictions, disappointments, joys, and sorrows that await them they know nothing. For reasons that a wise and merciful Father saw to be sufficient, he was pleased to withhold from the knowledge of mortals the events and incidents of their future days. But this he says to every one that will trust him: "I will guide thee with my counsel, and afterward receive thee to glory." This is enough.

But the future, dark and mysterious as it is, after all is but little more obscure and inexplicable than the past. Who in looking back over life is not compelled to confess that he has been led in a way that he had not known? Who has realized the hopes and expectations of his youth? Who has traveled the road he intended to travel? Who is this day what and where he intended to be ten or twenty years ago? Who is able to point out the precise cause that changed his course? See that young man, full of hope and expectation, as he looks into the future of life. He has had his youthful dreams, and sees little else before him but the most beautiful flowers. Not a thorn or a brier appears to his warm imagination. He says within himself, Now I shall have a most delightful journey. I see so many beautiful arbors where I shall sit down and rest, and be refreshed by the cooling waters and delicious fruits. But, alas! all at once, and without seeing any special cause for it, he is suddenly turned around, and is compelled by the force of unseen and unlooked-for events to travel over a rough and rugged way, until he is foot-sore and heart-sore. In his bewilderment and perplexity he sits down, ready to find fault with everything and everybody. Young man, there was a Father's eye upon you, and a hand unseen that guided your steps. He saw pit-falls and snares in the way you intended to go, that you did not see, into which you would have fallen if he had not turned your course. And now, instead of being what you are and where you are, you would be hopelessly ruined. When you have reached the end of your journey, rough and rugged as it may have been, and shall be permitted to review your life in the light of eternity, you will thank God most fervently that he thwarted your purposes and blighted the brightest dreams of your youth; yea, that he even blasted the tree from which you dreamed that you would eat such choice fruit in old age. You will then understand more fully the meaning of that scripture which affirms that "a man's heart deviseth his way, but the Lord directeth his steps."

Looking at the operations of divine providence,

they are often confused and entangled, because we are looking through a glass darkly. We see nothing clearly. We see the hand-writing on the wall, but can not interpret it. We see the burning bush, but know not its meaning. Dr. Fuller, said: "I looked upon the wrong or back side of a piece of arras (tapestry): it seemed to me as a continued nonsense. There was neither head nor foot therein. Confusion itself had as much method in it,—a company of thrums and threads, with many pieces and patches of several sorts, sizes, and colors; all of which signified nothing to my understanding. But then looking on the reverse, or right side thereof, all put together did spell excellent proportions, and figures of men and cities; so that, indeed, it was a history, not wrote with a pen, but wrought with a needle. If men look upon some of God's providential dealings with a mere eye of reason, they will hardly find any sense therein, such is their muddle and disorder. But, alas! the wrong side is objected to our eyes, while the right side is presented to the God of heaven, who knoweth that an admirable order doth result out of this confusion; and what is presented to him at present may, hereafter, be so showed to us as to convince our judgment in the truth thereof."

When God said to Abraham, "Get thee out of thy country, and from thy kindred, and from thy father's house, unto a land that I will show thee," it was all a mystery to him. Why it should be necessary for him to be separated from his kindred and native land, and go out into a strange country, he could not comprehend. Paul says that "when he was called to go out, immediately he obeyed, and went out, not knowing whither he went." He was compelled to walk in the shadow; but still he walked, because God commanded him. Such was his faith in the goodness, wisdom, and benevolence of God, that he would go forward no matter how dark the way might seem. Christians should learn from this, whether they comprehend the designs of God or not, whether the way is rough or smooth, light or dark, to go forward when God commands them to. There is nothing lost in obeying God. You can go anywhere in perfect safety if your Father says so.

"Had I but served my God with half the zeal
I served my king, He would not, in mine age,
Have left me naked to mine enemies."

It is truly marvelous to note the numerous instrumentalities through which and by which God operates in the execution of his plans. Kings, princes, and civil magistrates, whether they be good or bad men, are not unfrequently employed in the execution of his designs. Matter, whether animate or inanimate, is under his control and subject to his direction; he can use any or all of them as he pleases. And whatever comes to man through any of these agencies or instrumentalities, should be understood as coming by the command or special permission of God. God is eternal, immutable, omnipotent, omniscient, omnipresent, just, and holy. He can, if he choose, devise and execute his plans in the sight of men and angels; and if he choose, he can employ them in the execution of his plans without their knowledge of it. God has not placed himself under any obligations to either men or angels to communicate to them his designs. Trifling things are often made the hinges on which magnificent results turn. A boy enters a stable with a lighted lamp; it is accidently turned over, and in a short time a great city (Chicago) lies in ruins; millions of dollars worth of property is swept away; and a hundred thousand persons are sent out homeless. What the design of the Almighty was in suffering the great city to be burned we may not know. One thing is fixed as the eternal throne, that it will be overruled in such a way that greater good will result from it than could have been if the disaster had not befallen the city. How it will be brought about we may not be permitted to know. We know something of the history of that city up to the time of its burning, but what it would have been if no such calamity had befallen it, none can tell. God often interposes to prevent evil, and to save a people from utter ruin.

> "God is his own interpreter,
> And he will make it plain."

God said to Abraham, that in his seed all the nations of the earth should be blessed. In the fullness of time that son of promise was given. And when Isaac was grown up, God commanded Abraham to go to a certain mountain and offer him as a sacrifice. There is no reason to believe that Abraham knew anything about the purpose of the Almighty. To his mind it was all wrapped in profound mystery. God had given him the son according to promise, and in his (Isaac's) seed all the nations of the earth were to be blessed. But now to offer him as a sacrifice, while as yet he had no offspring, must have appeared very strange and mysterious. Nevertheless he went forward, and would have executed the command of God literally if there had been no interposition. Abraham believed God, and his faith carried him above the dust and must of human reason. He "knew that God's promise would march right forward to fulfillment." Abraham's faith never shone more brightly than when he stood over his boy with his arm raised to execute the command of God.

> "Though round him numerous tribes,
> Sworn foes to Heaven's dread rule, pitch their tents,
> No wayward doubts or coward fears appall
> The patriarch's soul. By the bright hope sustained,
> That in his seed all nations should be blest;
> Calm and unmoved the delegated seer
> Submissive bends to the eternal will."

In the prophet's vision of the living creatures attached to a curious vehicle, to which reference was made in a previous chapter, we have suggested the notion of mystery,—the wheels, living creatures, fire, rainbow, whirlwind, all compounded, moving forward and returning as lightning. When one went all went, notwithstanding the complication in the machinery. So in the operations of divine providence, there often appears a strange complication,—wheels turning this way and that way, some revolving backward and some forward, and yet the whole going straight forward. The wheels, which were full of eyes, were so bright that they were terrible to behold. So the plans of God are so vast that they reach from earth to heaven, from the beginning to the end of time, and streching far out into eternity; and this is one reason why the operations of Providence are often so mysterious to us. We see only in part; mere fragments of his operations; and can not tell how this or that movement of the wheels may be connected with other movements. And then, too, there is the appearance of a wheel in a wheel, which only increases the complication. As we look upon this vehicle, and see it moving with lightning speed, rolling as it were in fire,—and when the living creatures are lifted up the wheels are lifted up, while the spirit of the living creatures is in the wheels, all moving and returning as the spirit listeth,—we are ready to exclaim: "Oh, the depth of the riches both of the wisdom and knowledge of God. How unsearchable are his judgments, and his ways past finding out."

Afflictions and disappointments are sometimes just as necessary as health and prosperity, although we may not at the time be able to give any reason for it. God is watching all the time. He sees the way before us as distinctly as the way over which we have gone. If there are snares and pit-falls in advance of us our heavenly Father sees them, and may send afflictions or disappointments as messengers to turn us aside. We are weak and forgetful, and if God did not sometimes remind us of our frailty, we would seldom if ever think of it. The tired, worn travelers that appeared before Abraham's tent-door were angels in disguise. "Sickness takes us aside and sets us alone with God. We are taken into his private chamber, and there he converses with us face to face. The world is afar off, our relish for it is gone and we are alone with God. Many are the words of grace and truth which he then speaks to us. All our former props are struck away, and now we must lean on God alone. The things of earth are felt to be vanity; man's help is useless. Man's sympathy deserts us; we are cast wholly upon God, that we may learn that his praise and sympathy are enough. If it were not so, I should spend less time with God. If I had not been kept awake with pain I should have lost the sweetest experiences I ever had in my life. The disorder of my body is the very help I want from God; if it does its work before it lays me in the dust, it will raise me to heaven."

Blessings often come to us in disguise. They are angels unawares. But if properly entertained they will either hasten us out of the way of destruction or leave lasting blessing behind. "Why should I murmur?" said Henry Martyn, in his last sickness; "weakness, peril, and pain are but the ministering angels, whose office it is to conduct me to glory." Arrowsmith said, "Adversity, like winter weather, is of use to kill those vermin which the summer of prosperity is apt to produce and nourish." Rutherford said, "The wise Lord loves to feed us with hunger, and make us fat with wants and desertions." Moses Brown said, "A great deal of rust requires a rough file." Thus by ways and means, not our own choosing, the Lord manages to help us. Frederick the Great one day rang his bell several times, and no one came. He opened the door and found his page fast asleep. Approaching, intending to wake him, he saw the corner of a note hanging out of his pocket. He took the paper from his pocket, and, upon reading its contents, found it to be a letter from his mother. She was poor, and concluded the letter by assuring him that the Lord would bless him for his good conduct, and for sending home part of his pay. He returned the letter to the youth's pocket, and put with it a purse full of ducats. He then returned to his room, and rang his bell so loud that the page awoke and went in. "Thou hast slept well," said the king. The youth wished to excuse himself, and in the excitement of the moment thrust his hand into his pocket and felt the purse. He drew it out and, looking at the king, commenced to weep. "What is the matter?" asked the king. "O sire," said the page, "they wish to ruin me; I do not know how this money came into my pocket." "Why friend," said the king, "God often sends us blessings while we are asleep. Send that to your mother; salute her for me, and say that I will take care of thee."

Misfortunes are often wrongly interpreted. They are most generally set down as accidental, or sent as a punishment for some particular offense. A man, for instance, suddenly loses his property, or is disappointed in some important end he had hoped to gain. He sits down to grieve over it, never once thinking that it was all intended for his good. He does not see or believe that the hand of God was in it; that it was a link in the chain of events that would end in his highest good. To illustrate. A merchant in the city of New York failed in business: he gathered what was left and went to California. There he purchased land and built large mills. When all was completed, and he seemed to be just ready to regain his lost property, a heavy freshet swept everything away. Looking at the sad work, he was almost overcome with disappointment. The water had carried away the earth down to the rock, and uncovered a rich vein of gold. What he and all the rest had thought to be a great misfortune, turned out to his advantage. Thus in a thousand ways we misunderstand, and wrongly interpret, the operations of divine providence. Ordinarily "our worst misfortunes are those that never befall us."

"If friendless in a vale of tears I stray,
Where briers wound, and thorns perplex my way,—
Still let my steady soul thy goodness see,
And with strong confidence lay hold on thee;
With equal eye my various lot receive;
Resigned to die, or resolute to live;
Prepared to kiss the scepter or the rod,
While God is seen in all, and all in God."

From what we are permitted to know of the Divine perfections, it is very evident that however dark and mysterious God's ways may appear to us, they are intended for our highest good. Ten thousand events are transpiring every day about which we know little or nothing. Sometimes we see, or think we see, with considerable distinctness, then the whole scene changes, and we are lost in wonder and astonishment. "That mysterious suffering is not accidental—it is from God; but why and wherefore, and to what end, we know not. That severe stroke that swept from your eye the near, the dear, the beloved, is all wrapped in mystery. That storm that burst upon you like a thunder-bolt, and washed away the accumulation of the honest industry of many years, you see through a glass darkly. We know not what it is, nor whereto it tends. This only we know, that our God awakened the storm, our Father commissioned the cloud, and that what we do not see now we shall see hereafter, when we see no more through a glass darkly, but as face to face." If this "time haze" were to last forever; if the future had no bright to-morrow, we might well become sad and sorrowful. But this smoked medium, through which we are for the present compelled to look, will by and by pass away; the clouds will be scattered; the storms will have subsided; the trials and misfortunes of many long weary years will have ended; and from amid the brightness and glory of that everlasting day we may look back over life's stormy voyage and say, *Father, thou hast done all things well.*

Because the ways of providence are often dark and mysterious to us, we are not therefore to conclude that we are left to ourselves. God often leads his beloved by dark and intricate ways; not because he delights in afflicting and disappointing his children, but because he sees it is for their highest good. I doubt if anything save the immediate attraction of the cross of Jesus will appear more excellent to the saints in light, than the glory and wisdom of God's providences. The glorified saint, as he looks back over life's stormy way, will see how many times and for what purpose his course was unexpectedly changed. There at that place he will see how near he was to a horrible pit, and at that other place he was on the very brink of ruin. But the finger of God was there, and just in the nick of time caused his course to be changed. Ah! the redeemed will say, If my Father had not watched me all the time I should have been lost. They will realize more fully than ever before that he is all, in all things; that he was ever present, continually doing somewhat for their good.

Life is a state of discipline; and unless we could see and know what in every respect would assist in preparing us for a higher and holier state, and unless also we could see the end from the beginning, we are not in a condition to dictate to Infinite Wisdom what would be best for us. If Lot had been left to his own notions, he would doubtless have remained in Sodom. Two thoughts should be well impressed upon our minds. First: God is seeking to prepare us for himself, and whatever he does with us and by us points to that glorious end. Second: He seeks to accomplish by us and through us the greatest possible amount of good. Christians are not always compelled to walk in darkness and suffer on their own account. It was not for Abraham's sake alone that God commanded him to leave his native country. Others were to be benefited as well as himself. Jeremiah could have wept himself away for the sake of others.

"In the pilgrimage of this world, we know not whither we are going. The pillar of cloud which guides us is absolutely independent of our disposal. We must expect God's signals, and those indications which are properly called the leadings of his providences." It is folly for us to attempt to force a way in spite of providence, or attempt to throw off the yoke that is laid upon us. Jonah tried that experiment. We are so deplorably ignorant and short-sighted, that we can not tell what would be best for us; and we only exhibit our folly and weakness when we attempt to select our own way. We can not see how closely we are hedged in, nor how many threads there are in the loom of providence. God need not shake the mountains in order to change our course, a very little thing may do it; and out of a small matter God may bring the most stupendous results. There was nothing very remarkable in Joseph's going to see his brethren at Shechem, yet that was one thread in the web of events, that made him governor of Egypt. There was nothing extraordinary in the fact that the asses of Kish, the Benjaminite, should have strayed, yet that gave Israel a king; nothing out of the ordinary course of things, that David should visit his brethren at the camp in Elah, yet Goliath lost his head by it. In later times, it was but a small matter that a Dutchman should cut a few letters on the bark of a tree, and then transfer an impression of them on paper.

It was done for the amusement of children; but to this little event we trace the art of printing. That was a tiny vessel of only a hundred and eighty tons burden,—a mere speck, tossed on the angry waves of the Atlantic,—but in the hearts of the men that were on board that little nut-shell (the May Flower) was wrapped up the germ of all our free institutions, and a pure, evangelical, and free Christianity. Thus with individuals as well as nations, events are almost continually transpiring of which but little notice is taken at the time; and yet these are the pivots upon which the future destiny of men and nations turns.

> "O all-preparing Providence divine,
>   In thy large book, what secrets are enrolled,
> What sundry help doth thy great power assign,
>   To prop the course which thou intend'st to hold!
> What mortal sense is able to define
>   Thy mysteries, thy counsels manifold!
> It is thy wisdom strangely that extends
> Obscure proceedings to apparent ends."

It will often strengthen our hearts and give us courage to trust in God, if we remember that whilst his providences are often mysterious they are also universal, extending to everything, no matter how insignificant they may appear to us. Nothing in the universe—from the revolution of the planets to the delicate penciling of the lone flower in the wilderness—is left to the caprice of chance, or the iron rule of fate. God is everywhere, and everywhere at work. "We are in a labyrinth indeed, but the clew is in the hand of infinite wisdom and infinite love." The New Testament is full of paradoxes. Loss is gain; defeat is victory; sorrow is joy; weakness is strength; death is life; to go down is to go up. Thus in the mysterious leadings of providence, while we think we are going down we are going up; and when we are losing we are gaining. Often when pressed on every side by inexplicable mysteries, we do not know what to do, nor which way to turn our steps. Driven by unforeseen events, over which we can exercise no control, first to the right and then to left, we exclaim, in our perplexity and bewilderment, that "all these things are against me." How forcibly the language of Scripture comes to the mind under such strange circumstances. "Clouds and darkness are round about him: righteousness and judgment are the habitation of his throne." But thanks be to God, that from out of the thick clouds and darkness which hang around the throne words of cheer and comfort are spoken. "The Lord shall guide thee continually, and satisfy thy soul in drought, and make fat thy bones: and thou shalt be like a watered garden, and like a spring of water, whose waters fail not." "Fear thou not; for I am with thee: be not dismayed; for

I am thy God: I will strengthen thee; yea, I will help thee; yea, I will uphold thee with the right hand of my righteousness." "I will never leave thee, nor forsake thee." "When thou passest through the waters, I will be with thee; and through the rivers, they shall not overflow thee: when thou walkest through the fire, thou shalt not be burned; neither shall the flame kindle upon thee."

"So, Christian! though gloomy and sad be thy days,
    And the tempest of sorrow encompass thee black;
Though no sunshine of promise or hope shed its rays
    To illume and cheer thy life's desolate track;
Though thy soul writhes in anguish and bitter tears flow,
    O'er the wreck of fond joys, from thy bleeding heart riven,
Check thy murmuring sorrows, thou lone one, and know
    That the chastened on earth are the purest in heaven;
And remember, though gloomy thy present may be,
    That the Master is coming, and coming to thee."

CHAPTER IX.

CONSOLATION DERIVED FROM A BELIEF IN THE DOCTRINE OF PROVIDENCE. OMNISCIENCE, OMNIPOTENCE, AND OMNIPRESENCE OF GOD.

There is no theory, perhaps, with which the human mind grapples, more cold and repulsive than that Epicurean atheism which represents the Deity as inactive and unconcerned; that virtually dethrones and banishes him from his own creation. This cheerless sentiment, in its practical operations, is not confined to those who are known as skeptics, but may be found even among those professing Christianity. Our theology in the main is correct. Men everywhere say that they believe in a providence, and then practically deny it. I conceive that the ground of this practical skepticism lies in the failure to recognize a providence in little things. All perhaps allow that God is in the earthquake, the hurricane, and the fall of empires and kingdoms, but they fail to recognize his hand in the rain-drop, the snowflake, and the honey-comb. They imagine that it is easy enough to believe that the Creator can and does keep the sun, moon, and stars in their courses, but they can not understand how he can number the hairs of their heads, and notice the sparrow when it falls. It is too much for their faith to say that the great God, who spake worlds and systems into being, condescends to superintend the forming of every leaf and spire of grass.

Everything in the universe was so wisely arranged in the beginning that not anything new is created. New discoveries are being made; causes and forces in nature, which for many generations had been concealed, are being brought to light, but nothing new is originated. God created the heavens and the earth with all their hosts, together with all the laws and forces in nature, in six days, and pronounced the whole good and very good. The law of gravitation, the elastic power of steam, the force of electricity, were all there in the very morning of creation, but were not discovered until after many generations had passed away. So now there may yet be in nature laws and forces undiscovered. From what has been discovered, there is manifest the power, wisdom, and benevolence of the Creator, from the highest to the very lowest object in creation. Take up a plant, no matter how common it is, and you will observe in its structure a most wonderful correspondence of one thing to another. Examine the branches and leaves on the trees, the delicate penciling of the flowers, and you will see the most perfect order in everything,—the forms, shadings of color, lines, dots, niches, each in its proper place and in exact proportion. Now all this is the result, not of a new creation, but of a wise and perfect arrangement by the Creator in the beginning. Yet all these laws and forces, which produce these effects, are sustained by the power of God.

Rising above the plants and flowers we find the same power, wisdom, and benevolence of the Almighty exhibited in the creation of man. How complete, how wonderful is man.

"Mysterious link in being's endless chain,
Midway from nothing to the Deity."

The most enlightened philosophy of the present day recognizes as true the historical fact that man came upon earth, not by a succession of beings, but by a direct creation. "None of the researches of geology," says Mr. Hitchcock, "in any part of the globe, have succeeded in bringing to light one single fragment of the fossilized frame of man in any undisturbed geological formation. Thus, then, the new and brilliant science of geology attests that man was the last of created beings on this planet. If her data are consistent and true, and worthy of scientific consideration, she affords conclusive evidence that, as we are told in Scripture, he can not have occupied the earth longer than six thousand years."

There have been many attempts among philosophers and poets to describe the generic character of man. Some descriptions are wise, and some exceedingly foolish. Plato describes man "as a two-legged animal without feathers." And it is said that Socrates brought a cock despoiled of his feathers into Plato's school, and exclaimed, "Behold the man of Plato." Franklin calls man "a tool-making animal." Walker calls him "a cultivating animal." Hazlitt calls man "a poetical animal." Adam Smith calls man "an animal that makes bargains." But laying all such partial descriptions of man aside, we see in his organization, physically, mentally, and morally, a most wonderful display of wisdom, power, and goodness. We find in him a capacity for improvement and happiness; and in looking around we find that all the necessary means for the proper development of all his faculties and powers have been provided and placed within his reach; so that if men are not happy it is because they refuse to use the means provided for that end.

In whatever direction we choose to look, we see unmistakable evidences of wisdom and goodness.

Unity and design are exhibited in the composition and adjustment of everything. There is also a uniformity, and at the same time an almost endless variety. All things in this beautiful and harmonious arrangement are governed by general laws. "But the plan, as it is devised by divine wisdom, requires divine wisdom to execute it." We must not suppose, however, because a wise and benevolent God created all things, and established general laws by which they are to be controlled, that therefore these laws will execute their purposes independently. We have said elsewhere, and repeat it in this connection, that there is not a law in the universe, either natural, mental, physical, or moral, but would instantly become inoperative if the presence and power of God were withdrawn. "The painter's soul is no doubt thrown into his painting, and the sculptor's and architect's into their statues and buildings; but their souls meanwhile exist apart, and are capable of other acts besides these. In a sense as true as it is grand, the soul of the Creator is streaming through the order and life of creation; but meanwhile he exists independent of and far above them."

But we are in this chapter more especially to consider some of the sources of comfort and consolation arising from a belief in the doctrine of an all-pervading providence, as taught in the Holy Scriptures,—not a belief in God's superintendence of certain great events in nature, nor that he is more especially drawn toward great men, but that he in the beginning foresaw whatsoever would occur and provided for it; also, that he is everywhere present to sustain and control all laws and events in the kingdom of nature and grace; that he directs the steps of the good man, and overrules the evil designs and acts of wicked men; in a word, that he is almighty, and doeth all things according to the counsel of his own will.

The first source of comfort to which we call attention is a firm, unyielding faith in the omniscience of the Almighty. That he is all-wise is as clearly revealed in the Holy Scriptures as that he exists. "With him is wisdom and strength, he hath counsel and understanding?" Job xii. 13. "He that planted the ear, shall he not hear? he that formed the eye, shall he not see?" Ps. xciv. 9. All things are known unto him. He knoweth himself, his nature, and perfections. He knoweth all his creatures,—*all are manifest in his sight.* Heb. iv. 13. All things, whether animate or inanimate, are known to him. He knows the tiny flower that blooms and fades alone in the wilderness. He knows the insect that reposes on the rose-leaf, as well as Michael the archangel.

Thales being asked whether a man doing ill could lie hid to or be concealed from God, answered, "No, nor thinking neither." Pindon says, "If any man hopes that anything will be concealed from God he is deceived."

The marks of God, everywhere in his wide domain, show the wisdom of their author. Oh, the depth both of the wisdom and knowledge of God, displayed in arranging and providing for a universe so complicated, and yet so harmoniously connected that every one arrangement moves in exact harmony with every other arrangement. What a wise combination of wheels working in wheels was necessary in order to supply the wants of every living thing. The seed of a certain plant may be necessary to sustain the life of a bird, while the root supplies the wants of a worm. Now all this must have been seen and provided for when the plan of the universe was laid. The end must have been seen from the beginning, as well as the result of every law, and combination of laws. Thus the whole machinery of nature moves on without a single jar,—cause producing effects, and these again producing other effects.

Let the student of nature consider but a few things, and he will be forced to conclude that the arrangements in nature are so ample and complete as to defy the power and wisdom of man to have devised. Take for example the sunbeam, composed, it is said, of three different principles,—the chemical, luminiferous, and caloric. The first has a wonderful influence in germinating plants; the second assists in secreting from the atmosphere the necessary amount of carbon, and the third is necessary to nurture the seed, and form the reproductive elements. Again, if the air did not possess an undulating quality we should be deprived of all the advantages of speech and conversation, and of all the pleasures of music. Take another view. Creatures that burrow in the ground have bodies shaped like a wedge. Animals that live in the artic regions are clothed in fir. Birds are provided with hollow bones and a downy covering suited to float in the air. And thus, if we were disposed to continue the investigation, we should find in every department of nature the same wise and benevolent arrangement. Dr. McCosh says, "When we believe that there is such a being, we feel as if all were safe and secure; for we know that there never can be derangement in works planned by infinite wisdom, and protected by an everywhere present and ever watchful guardian. Such a faith will impart a holy courage even to the most timid; we feel as if we might be unharmed amid the conflagration of worlds, and while the visible universe is passing away."

It would not seem to require an extraordinary amount of credulity to believe that He who so wisely and graciously planned the universe, with all its complication and harmony, should have included in that wise and perfect arrangement all the necessary provisions for the present and future happiness of man. Men lay their plans for the future, and enter upon their execution without knowing what the result will be. They can not see into the future, and hence can not provide against emergencies. They may provide for one class of events, but disaster may come from an opposite direction. But when God in his wisdom planned the universe, he saw the end from the beginning, with every possible and conceivable event that could or would occur. He saw as well what the raven would need as what man would need, and hence was able to provide for everything. God can not be surprised, as men are surprised.

> "A thousand nameless acts,
> That lurk in lonely secrecy, and die,
> Unnoticed, like the trodden flowers which fall
> Beneath the proud man's foot, to Thee are known,
> And written, with a sunbeam, in the book
> Of life, where Mercy fills the brightest page."

A firm, Abrahamic-like faith in God will bring us into such connection and union with him, and give us such clear conceptions of his wisdom in arranging and providing for the final good of man, that nothing will be able to separate us from his love. Every possible event of life was foreseen and provided for. No wind can blow wrong. Even sorrows and afflictions, together with the most cruel disappointments, can only help to set "some luminous jewel of joy" in our future crown. "Our very mourning shall be but the enamel around the diamond; our very hardships but the metallic rim that holds the opal, glancing with strange interior fire." Because "the violinist screws up the key till the tense cord sounds the concert pitch," we are not to suppose that he intends to destroy it; neither are we to suppose that because God turns us around he therefore intends to destroy us. The violinist knows what each cord can bear; so God will not allow his beloved to be overburdened.

Another source of comfort arises from a settled conviction of the power of God. It not only required infinite wisdom to devise the plan for such a stupendous work as that of creation and redemption, but it also required unlimited power to execute the plan. This attribute may very readily be inferred if we consider, in the light of Scripture, the infinity, independence, and perfections of the Divine Character. The works of creation and redemption are standing witnesses of his eternal power. "Ah Lord God! behold, thou hast made the heaven and the earth by thy great power and stretched out arm, and there is nothing too hard for thee." Jer. xxxii. 17. "God hath spoken once; twice have I heard this; that power belongeth unto God." Ps. lxii. 11. "And all the inhabitants of the earth are reputed as nothing: and he doeth according to his will in the army of heaven, and among the inhabitants of the earth: and none can stay his hand, or say unto him, What doest thou?" Dan. iv. 35. The power of God is not only exhibited in the creation of the universe, but also in the sustenation of all things. "For in him we live, and move, and have our being; as certain also of your own poets have said, For we are also his offspring." Acts xvii. 28. "Thou, even thou, art Lord alone; thou hast made heaven, the heaven of heavens, with all their host, the earth, and all things that are therein, the seas, and all that is therein, and thou preservest them all." Neh. ix. 6. "He upholdeth all things by the word of his power." The saints in heaven were heard to say, "The Lord God omnipotent reigneth."

The power of God is as gloriously manifest in the blessed work of redemption as it is in the creation and sustenation of all things. It was a sublime act to speak worlds and systems into being, and send them whirling through space, but "'twas greater to redeem." "Man," says J. B. Brown, "and all things were made in concert, to form part of the same great system, of which man's life was to be the key-note, and man himself was to be the head. And the whole system, the whole structure of man and the world, is molded to be the theater of the redemption of the sinner,—not in Eden, but on Calvary; and in heaven, which is the child of Calvary, we see realized the whole idea of God." In Adam all was lost. The law was broken, and all the powers of darkness seemed bent on the endless ruin of man. But God, through the infinity of his eternal love, interposed, and in his wisdom devised and by his power executed a plan by which, and in which, he could be just, and yet save those that were lost.

What a firm ground for consolation there is in this. He who created all things and redeemed a world that was lost, is my Father and friend. Weary, tired one, is not that power by which the universe was made, and by which it is now sustained, sufficient to sustain thee? Can not he who beareth up the pillars of heaven bear thee up also. Can not he by whose almighty power Arcturus and his sons are still kept circling around the pole keep thee from falling? Is not he who executed all his wise designs in creation and redemption able to execute all his designs in reference to thyself? Is there a weapon formed against thee that can prevail, since God is thy shield? Can any one find thee since thy life is hid with Christ in God? Can any power on the earth or under it crush thee down, seeing that God hath said, "I will uphold thee with the right hand of my righteousness?" Can any part of the road be too dark and difficult, since God has said, "Fear thou not, for I am with thee?" Can any affliction be too severe, since God has said, "I will never leave thee, nor forsake thee?" Can any burden be too heavy, since God has invited thee to cast all thy care upon him? Can any mountain be too steep to climb, or river too broad to cross, since God has said, I will lead thee? Beloved, there is nothing that ought to excite either your fear or your dread. Paul says: "Neither death, nor life, nor angels, nor principalities, nor powers, nor things present, nor things to come, nor hight, nor depth, nor any other creature, shall be able to separate us from the love of God, which is in Christ Jesus our Lord." Rom. viii. 38, 39. "He is able to save to the uttermost." Christian, if at any time the way becomes dark and difficult; if rugged mountains rise before thee; if thou shouldst come even to the bank of some wide ocean; if then the hosts of darkness should come in like a flood, stand still, and thou shalt see and feel the salvation of God. "Lo, these are parts of his ways; but how little a portion is heard of him? but the thunder of his power who can understand?" Job xxvi. 14.

> "What is too great, if we the cause survey?
> Stupendous Architect, thou, thou art all!
> My soul flies up and down in thought of thee—
> And finds herself but at the center still!
> I AM, thy name! existence all thine own!
> Creation's nothing: flattered much, if styled
> The thin, the fleeting atmosphere of God."

The omnipresence of God furnishes substantial ground for lasting consolation. This blessed truth is very clearly and forcibly taught in the Holy Scriptures. "Can any hide himself in secret places that I shall not see him? saith the Lord. Do not I fill heaven and earth? saith the Lord." Jer. xxiii. 24. "But will God indeed dwell on the earth? behold, the heaven and heaven of heavens can not contain thee." I. Kings viii. 27. God is everywhere, in all places at the same time. Nothing, however minute it may be, can transpire without his notice. One in ancient times said, "*Thou, God, seest me.*" Consider the individualism in this declaration—not the world in general, not kings and princes only, not my neighbor, not my friends, but, "Thou, God, seest ME."

Ah, "whither shall I go from thy Spirit? or whither shall I flee from thy presence? If I ascend up into heaven, thou art there: if I make my bed in hell, behold, thou art there. If I take the wings of the morning, and dwell in the uttermost parts of the sea; even there shall thy hand lead me, and thy right hand shall hold me." Ps. cxxxix. 7–10.

The doctrine of the omnipresence of God, while it is a source of deep and lasting consolation to the hearts of all good men, should awaken in the minds of all evil doers deep and solemn considerations. If God is everywhere at the same time, then every thought, purpose, and act is open to his inspection. Men may throw about them the myterious garb of secrecy; they may select the most secluded spot on earth, and hide from the eyes of men; but the eye of God is upon them. At every step they are God-inclosed. Every thought and purpose of the heart is as well known to God as if it were in seven-fold thunder proclaimed on the mountain top. "The cloud on the mountain is his covering; the muttering from the chambers of the thunder is his voice; that sound on the top of the mulberrry-trees is his 'going;' in that wind, which bends the forest or curls the clouds, he is walking; that sun is his still commanding eye." During the American war. as a

British officer was walking out early one morning he saw an old man whom he supposed was taking aim at some object. He approached him, and asked what he was about. The old man waved his hand, by which he expressed a desire to be let alone. Presently the officer approached closer, and taking him by the arm said, "You old fool, what are you doing?" The old man said, "I am worshiping the Great Spirit." The officer then asked where the Great Spirit was to be found. To which the native replied, "Soldier, *where* is he not?"

The omnipresence of God to a Christian is a fountain of pleasure. All his trials, temptations, persecutions, afflictions, losses, and weaknesses are known to him. He sees every effort he makes to do good and to be good; he is present to help in every time of need; he is present to direct the steps of a good man, and to control and overrule surrounding events. When Jesus said to his disciples, "Lo, I am with you alway," he meant more than that he would be with them as an ordinary traveling companion. "I am with you alway," to direct your steps, control events, to open the way before you, defend and help you at all times and in all places. So he is with his people—with every member of his flock, no matter how poor and obscure he may be. An old lady, living in an out of the way cabin, was one day visited by her pastor. When the good man entered the house and saw how destitute she was, he said, "Good woman, you are very poor." "Sir," said she, "you see that I have but little of this world's goods, but depend upon it I have Jesus with me." He was with the Hebrews in the furnace, with Daniel in the lions' den, with the apostles in prison, with John on the island of Patmos, with the martyrs in the flames. Nothing can befall one of the least of his family without his notice; yea, more, nothing can befall them without his permission. "A company of poor Christians," says Dr. Spencer, "were banished into some remote parts; and one standing by, seeing them pass along, said, 'that it was a very sad condition those poor people were in, to be thus hurried from the society of men and to be made companions with the beasts of the field.' 'True,' said another, 'it were a sad condition indeed, if they were carried to a place where they should not find their God. But let them be of good cheer, God goes along with them, and will exhibit the comforts of his presence wherever they go. He is an infinite God and filleth all places.'"

I conceive that when a Christian has clear conceptions of the omnipresence of the Almighty, and a conscious conviction within that he is trying to do the best he can, he will be contented with his lot in life, be it ever so trying. Afflictions, sorrows, and disappointments may come, but the good man realizes that it is all under the eye of his Father. He will feel somewhat as St. Augustine did when he said, "Behold us willing to suffer in this life the worst it may please thee to bring upon us; here lay thy rod upon us; 'consume us here, cut us to pieces here, only spare us in eternity.'" A mother gave her two little ones some books and toys with which to amuse themselves, while she went up stairs to do some work. Sometime after the mother was gone, a timid voice from the foot of the stairs called out, "Mamma, are you there?" "Yes, darling." "All right then," said the little voice, and the child went back to her books and toys. A little while after, the same question came from the foot of the stairs, "Mamma, are you there?" "Yes, dear." "All right then," responded the little child, and they resumed their play, feeling that all was well. Thus God's little ones, in their loneliness, may look up by faith and ask, "My Father, art thou there? And when there comes the assurance of his presence their hearts may be quieted." When Jacob awoke from his sleep, and remembered his vision, he exclaimed, "Surely, God was in this place and I knew it not."

Paul, in his Epistle to the Hebrews, says, "Be content with such things as ye have, for he hath said, *I will never leave thee, nor forsake thee.*" Here we have a positive affirmation that God will be ever present; and, as we have already said, this divine presence with his people means more than that general presence which is extended equally to all. It implies that he will be present to uphold and help whenever and wherever it is necessary. It implies that "whatever there is in God of help and comfort is herein made over to the believer through Christ. It contains provision for body and for soul in life, in death, and in eternity. It covers every instance, addresses itself to every character, and meets every emergency." But the promise of the Father to be ever present does not necessarily exempt the believer from afflictions and trials. This is neither taught nor implied. "In the world," said Jesus, "ye shall have tribulation." But the promise, while it does not exempt from the ills of life, is nevertheless full and complete, and secures to the believer all the help he will need. The winds may howl tempestuously about him, the earth may be shaken under him, the thunders may crash above him, his helm may be broken, and his sail rent in twain, until in his bewilderment he may cry out, with one of old, "All these things are against me." He may be brought into perils, and even into thick darkness, until, with the psalmist, he exclaims, "All thy billows and thy waves have gone over me." But at such times he may with the utmost confidence look heavenward and say, "My Father, hast thou not said, 'I will never leave thee nor forsake thee?'"

God has not said to you, brother or sister, that you should never go through fire and flood; but he did say, blessed be his name, "When thou passest through the waters I will be with thee, and through the rivers, they shall not overflow thee." He has not said that you should never be an orphan, but he authorized you to say, "When my father and my mother forsake me, then the Lord will take me up." He did not tell you that you should not be afflicted, but he did say that "our light affliction, which is but for a moment, worketh for us a far more exceeding and eternal weight of glory." He did not say that you should not be tempted, but he did say that you should not be "tempted above that ye are able," and with the temptation there should be a way to escape. He did not say that you should never get old, but he did say, "Even to your old age I am he; and even to hoar hairs will I carry you: I have made, and I will bear; even I will carry, and will deliver you." He did not say that you should not be persecuted, but he did say, "Blessed are they which are persecuted for righteousness' sake: for theirs is the kingdom of heaven." He did not say that you should have the honors of this world, but Jesus said, "If any man serve me, him will my Father honor." When Polycarp was asked to deny the truth, he answered, "Eighty and six years have I served my Savior, and he hath never done me any harm; and shall I deny him now?" Wilberforce remarked, "I can scarcely understand why my life is spared so long, except it is to show that a man can be as happy without a fortune as with one." Soon after, when his only daughter died, he wrote, "I have often heard that sailors on a voyage will drink 'friends astern' till they are half-way over, then 'friends ahead.' With me it has been 'friends ahead' this long time." Happy in old age, because God is present to uphold with the right hand of his righteousness. A stranger said to Mr. Venn, "Sir, I think you are on the wrong side of fifty." "On the wrong side of fifty?" said Mr. Venn. "No, sir; I am on the right side of fifty." "Surely," the stranger replied, "you must be turned fifty?" "Yes, sir," added Mr. Venn, "but I am on the right side of fifty; for every year I live I am nearer my crown of glory."

Once in a while as the storms incident to human life burst with all their pent-up fury upon the Christian's head, he may exclaim, with Rachel, "I am weary of life," or with David, "Oh that I had wings like a dove, for then would I fly away and be at rest." He may be compelled to walk in darkness. To his mind the mystic wheels of divine providence are turning backward. At such times, from out of the thick clouds which are around the throne, a voice may be heard—it is the voice of God: "For a small moment have I forsaken thee; but with great mercies will I gather thee. In a little wrath I hid my face from thee for a moment; but with everlasting kindness will I have mercy on thee, saith the Lord thy Redeemer." "For the mountains shall depart, and the hills be removed; but my kindness shall not depart from thee, neither shall the covenant of my peace be removed, saith the Lord, that hath mercy on thee." How unreasonable, then, in the face of such assurances, for a Christian to doubt or be in the least intimidated. Every possible condition in which he may be placed is completely hedged in by promises, for every step of his way was foreseen and provided for; every nook and corner, every temptation, sorrow, and affliction was arranged for in the most ample manner. The whole journey has been strewed with living promises, and God, by his almighty power and universal presence, is abundantly able to execute all the plans his wisdom devised. Gotthold remarked that the world was like an ocean, on which most of the mariners are shipwrecked in pleasant weather. "On this ocean I am steering my little bark. Be with me, O my God, and guide me to the wished-for shore. It will matter little then whether I sailed in calm and sunshine, or through storms and tempests." St. Chrysostom, who suffered under the Empress Eudoxia, told his friend Cyricus how he had armed himself beforehand. "I thought," said he, "will she banish me? 'The earth is the Lord's and the fullness thereof.' Take away my goods? Naked came I into the world, and naked must I return. Will she stone me? I remembered Stephen. Behead me? John the Baptist came into my mind."

A Christian has nothing within himself of which he can boast; but when firmly planted upon the rock of God's wisdom, power, and universal presence, he can be calm and composed. Let the great wheels of providence turn as they will, fast or slow, backward or forward, it is God that causes them to revolve. If I do not and can not understand the workings of the cogs in the wheels, my Father does. If I can only see in part, my Father sees it all; and in due time I shall see as I am seen.

> "Father, oh with patience bless us,
> Till each seeming ill be past;
> Let whatever gloom oppress us,
> All must end in light at last."

CHAPTER X.

CONSOLATION ARISING FROM A BELIEF IN THE DOCTRINE OF PROVIDENCE—CONTINUED. IMMUTABILITY, JUSTICE, AND VERACITY OF GOD.

In the preceding chapter we endeavored to demonstrate the fact that the wisdom, power, and omnipresence of God were all directly connected with the government of the universe, and were all pledged to secure for man the highest possible good; and that because these perfections of the divine nature were so closely allied, and so inseparably connected with every conceivable event in life, it therefore formed a source of lasting consolation to the hearts of all who trusted in God. Whether God could have flung a world from the finger of his omnipotence, and sent it whirling in its orbit, so constituted that there should have been nothing but a few general laws, and those laws entirely free from all complexity, so that all coming events could have been reckoned with as much certainty as the astronomer reckons the time of an eclipse, is not for us to say. Certain it is that we are not placed in any such world.

There are some general laws by which some things are so governed that both the cause and the effect may be seen and well understood. The astronomer can tell the very minute of an eclipse ten or twenty years before its occurrence; but he can not tell what will be on the morrow. Whether it will rain or shine, whether he will be sick or well, living or dying, he can not tell. The events of life in the future are for the most part all locked up—an unsolved problem. How reasonable then is the doctrine of providence, which includes not only those general ideas, but every minute particular. In the design, creation, and sustenation of all things, we see most beautifully blended the power, wisdom, and omnipresence of the Creator.

In this chapter we propose to consider other attributes and perfections of the Divine Character, as they stand connected with the government of the universe, and from which Christians may derive strength and comfort under the most trying circumstances in life. If Christians knew more about the attributes and perfections of the Divine Being, as they are revealed in the Holy Scriptures, they would see more in him to revere, and love, and trust. There is enough in God to meet and satisfy every want of the soul for time and eternity. Bishop Hall, when speaking of the fullness of God, says: "Though numberless drops be in the sea, yet if one be taken out of it it hath so much the less, though insensibly; but God, because he is infinite, can admit of no diminution. Therefore are men niggardly, because the more they give the less they have. But thou, Lord, mayst give what thou wilt without abatement of thy store. Good prayers never come weeping home. I am sure I shall receive either what I ask or what I should ask." He that hath God hath all things. Paul said to Christians in his day, and to us as well: "For all things are yours; whether Paul, or Apollos, or Cephas, or the world, or life, or death, or things present, or things to come; all are yours; and ye are Christ's; and Christ is God's. I. Cor. iii. 21–23. "Take a pen," says Dr. Spencer, "and write down riches, honors, preferments, they are all but as so many ciphers; they signify nothing; but write down God alone, and he will raise them to thousands, hundreds of thousands. And then it is that a Christian is truly happy,—when he can find in himself and all things in his God."

>"The soul reposing on assured relief,
>Feels herself happy amidst all her grief;
>Forgets her labor as she toils along,
>Weeps tears of joy, and bursts into a song."

The first grounds of consolation we shall consider in this connection is the immutability of God. This attribute he claims as peculiar to himself. "I am the Lord, I change not." Mal. iii. 6. "The counsel of the Lord standeth forever, the thoughts of his heart to all generations." Ps. xxxiii. 11. "Every good gift and every perfect gift is from above, and cometh down from the Father of lights, with whom is no variableness, neither shadow of turning." Jas. i. 17. Mutability belongs to creatures, but not to the Creator. Man, even in his best estate, was mutable and fell. Angels in their original purity were mutable and liable to change, and did apostatize. 'Good men are mutable and sometimes fall. God alone is immutable. "I am the Lord, I change not." He is the same yesterday, to-day, and forever. He is unchangeable in his nature, attributes, perfections, and purposes. He is unchangeable in his love, promises, and threatenings.

This perfection in the divine nature, more perhaps than any other of his attributes, distinguishes him from human nature. And on account of this divine perfection, order, harmony, and steadfastness are maintained in the universe of matter and mind. If God were changeable as men, or even as angels are, there would be but little uniformity in his government, and no security whatever in his promises. What God has said that he will do. The heavens may pass away, the moon and stars may fall, and the earth dissolve, but his word must and will stand unmoved forever. "The grass may wither, the flower fade, but the word of the Lord shall endure forever." A minister, in his pastoral work, visited a pious but poor woman, and during his stay noticed that her Bible was marked at different places with the letters T and P. Not knowing what this might mean, he asked the good woman to explain. "Oh," said she, "those are the promises in my precious Bible. There are many of them, you see, I have tried; so I marked them T; and many I have proved, and I know that they are true, so I marked them P." "Promises," says Spurstowe, "are like bonds, which depend altogether upon the sufficiency of the surety. If a beggar seal an instrument for the payment of ten thousand pounds, who esteems it to be any better than a blank? But if a man of estate and ability do bind himself to pay such a sum, it is looked upon as so much real estate; and men value themselves by such bills and bonds as well as by what is in their own possession. God, who hath made such rich promises to believers, is able to perform what he hath spoken."

An objection is sometimes urged against the idea of God's immutability on this ground. It is said, for example, that the wrath of God abideth on the wicked; but suppose that that wicked man should repent and turn from his wickedness, then the wrath of God toward him would cease. Yes, this is a blessed truth. There is in this a change in the divine administration toward the sinner relatively, but there is no change in the principles of the administration; that is immutable. It is fixed as the eternal throne to treat all characters the same. There is a change, not in the administration of the law, but in the subject of the law. Man unregenerated is under the condemnation of the law, but when he repents and turns to God he is received under the protection of the law. Christ met and fully satisfied the claims of the law by his death on the cross; hence Paul says, "There is therefore now no condemnation to them which are in Christ Jesus." The law remains forever the same, condemning all who are out of Christ, and justifying all who are in Christ. "God is immutably determined to give or withhold blessings accordingly." He has declared once for all and forever that the wicked (character) shall perish; and the righteous (character) shall be saved. Men may change in their relation to the law, but the law is immutable. One passage of scripture on this point will suffice: "Therefore, thou son of man, say unto the children of thy people, The righteousness of the righteous shall not deliver him in the day of his transgression: as for the wickedness of the wicked, he shall not fall thereby in the day that he turneth from his wickedness; neither shall the righteous be able to live for his righteousness in the day that he sinneth. When I shall say to the righteous, that he shall surely live; if he trust to his own righteousness, and commit iniquity, all his righteousness shall not be remembered; but for his iniquity that he hath committed, he shall die for it. Again, when I say unto the wicked, Thou shalt surely die; if he turn from his sin, and do that which is lawful and right; if the wicked restore the pledge, give again that he had robbed, walk in the statutes of life, without committing inquity; he shall surely live, he shall not die." Ezekiel xxxiii. 12–15. From what is here taught we can not fail to see that the ways of God are equal, and that it is immutably fixed (not decreed) that the righteous (character) shall be saved and the wicked (character) shall perish.

To illustrate still further the immutability of God: He has said that "the saints of the Most High shall take the kingdom, and possess it forever and ever." And so it shall be. God has not immutably determined who shall be the saints; all may be if they will; but the saints, whoever they may be, shall have the kingdom. No matter how poor and despised among men they may be; no matter what their trials and conflicts may be. Their way through life may be ever so dark and rugged; all the powers of earth and hell may rise against them—God has said that they shall have the kingdom; and so it will be, though the heavens fall. "Oh, I wonder," asks the desponding saint, "whether I shall ever be saved?" You need not wonder at all. If you "trust in the Lord and do good," you have the promise which can not fail. "But the way is so dark and difficult." No matter, since God has said that he would be with you to uphold and strengthen you. He has made all the necessary provisions for your journey, and has thrown up a way which is above the common ways of life, and not one jot or tittle of his word shall fail. His own words are these: "God is not a man, that he should lie; neither the son of man, that he should repent: hath he said, and shall he not do it? or hath he spoken, and shall he not make it good?" Num. xxiii. 19. God is allwise, and therefore would not promise what he could not make good. He is omnipotent, and is therefore able to do all that he promised. He is immutable, and therefore must do all he has said. From these attributes and perfections of the Divine Character, the Christian may draw constant satisfaction. Faith in God is the lever that often turns darkness into light. A poor little orphan boy asked a lady, one cold day, to permit him to clean away the snow from her steps. "Do you get much to do?" asked the lady. "Sometimes I do," was answered, "but often I get very little." "Are you not then afraid that you will not get enough to live on?" "Don't you think," said the boy, "that God will take care of me, if I put my trust in him and do the best I can?" Some naturalists desired to obtain some beautiful flowers that grew on the side of a dangerous precipice in the Scotch Highlands. They offered a boy a considerable sum of money if he would descend by a rope and secure them. He looked at the money and then at the danger, and replied, "I will go down, if my father will hold the rope." Here is faith, simple and unwavering. Are we not as safe in the hands of the immutable God as that little boy was in the hands of his father?

> "The steps of Faith
> Fall on the seeming void, and find
> The rock beneath."

Another source of comfort is the justice of God. This is that perfection of his nature "whence arises the absolute rectitude of his moral government," by which equal laws are prescribed and equal rewards and punishments are dispensed. Justice, as an attribute, is not independent of the other attributes and perfections, but acts in harmony with them. God is just in and of himself. Man may be just according to some established rule or law, but God has no law without himself. He is just in his very nature, independent of all law, and is the source of all justice. This perfection of the divine nature has been distinguished into remunerative and punitive justice. The former implies a proper distribution of rewards, and the latter implies the infliction of punishment for wrong-doing. Caussin, when speaking of justice and mercy, says that "justice and mercy are the two arms of God which embrace, bear, and govern the whole world; they are the two engines of the great Archimedes, which make heaven descend upon earth and earth mount up to heaven. They are the bass and treble strings of the great lute of heaven, which make all the harmonies and tunable symphonies of this universe. Now as mercy is infinite, so is justice. The divine essence holdeth these two perfections as the two scales of the balance, always equally poised."

The justice of God is so clearly taught in the Holy Scriptures that we need only refer to a few passages. "He is the Rock, his work is perfect: for all his ways are judgment: a God of truth and without iniquity, just and right is he." Deut. xxxii. 4. "Justice and judgment are the habitation of thy throne: mercy and truth shall go before thy face." Ps. lxxxix. 14. "There is no God else beside me; a just God and a Savior." Isa. xlv. 21. "Who will render to every man according to his deeds." Rom. ii. 6.

It being well established from the Holy Scriptures that God is just in his nature, it will not be difficult to understand and believe that he is, and will be, just in his administration of all the affairs of his government. He is just in all his works and ways, and will ultimately render to every man according to his works. The queen of France, Anne of Austria, said to her enemy, Cardinal Richelieu: "My lord cardinal, there is one fact which you seem to have entirely forgotten. God is a sure paymaster. He may not pay at the end of every week, or month, or year; but I charge you remember that he pays in the end." God is just in all the operations of his providences. Uncertain, inexplicable, and unequal as some of his ways may appear to us now, it is fixed as the eternal throne that justice will be meted out to every one in the end. "Say ye to the righteous, that it shall be well with him: for they shall eat the fruit of their doings. Woe unto the wicked! it shall be ill with him: for the reward of his hands shall be given him." Is. iii. 10, 11. In the past, more especially than now, God permitted his beloved ones to be severely dealt with. Many of them were most cruelly tortured and put to death. God saw it all and permitted it to be so.

> "The sun of justice may withdraw his beams
> Awhile from earthly ken, and sit concealed
> In dark recess, pavilioned round with clouds;
> Yet let not guilt presumptuous rear her crest,
> Nor virtue droop despondent; soon these clouds,
> Seeming eclipse, will brighten into day,
> And in majestic splendor he will rise,
> With healing and with terror on his wing."

Complicated and mysterious as the revolutions of the wheels of providence may now appear to our beclouded vision, "the Judge of the whole earth will do right." When the celestial gates of paradise were opened to John, on the island of Patmos, he saw, among other things, a great multitude standing on what seemed to him to be a sea of glass mingled with fire. They were such as had gotten the victory over the beast, and over his mark, and over the number of his name. And as he gazed upon them he heard them "sing the song of Moses the servant of God, and the song of the Lamb, saying, Great and marvelous are thy works, Lord God Almighty; just and true are thy ways, thou King of saints." From this lofty eminence in the better land they may have been retrospecting the past—looking over the way they had traveled. Perhaps, while in the conflicts of life, they had sometimes thought and felt as

Christians now think and feel—that the balances were not always kept even. But now, seeing the past in a clearer light and from a very different stand-point, and being made acquainted with the designs and purposes of God, they could feel and say that his ways were just and righteous altogether.

It is often very difficult for even the best of Christians to understand how it is that God is no respecter of persons. One is raised up and another is put down; one amasses wealth and another remains poor; one seems to glide along smoothly and easily, whilst another is full of trouble and sorrow. David was for awhile severely tempted over this seeming partiality, especially when he considered the prosperity of the wicked. "I was envious at the foolish, when I saw the prosperity of the wicked. For there are no bands in their death: but their strength is firm. They are not in trouble as other men. * * * Their eyes stand out with fatness: they have more than heart could wish." Ps. lxxiii. 3–5, 7. David was sorely pressed in spirit, and ready to find fault with the divine administration. It seemed to his beclouded mind that the dispensations of God's providences were unequal, and that this was incompatible with the eternal principles of justice. In this complaint he seems even to doubt the very existence of

Providence. The wicked were better off than the righteous; they had all, and even more than heart could wish. Then they had no bands in their death. In a word, the ungodly had it better than the godly, and there was no advantage in trying to be good. These were some of his reflections; and as he thus looked upon men from a human stand-point, he became disquieted in spirit, and his feet well-nigh slipped. David was not the first nor the last man that took such a gloomy view of God's providential dealing with the children of men. But when he went into the sanctuary and consulted with God, as good men always should do, his spiritual horizon was cleared up, and he was straightway relieved from all his anxiety. When he considered the future state of the righteous and wicked, in connection with their present state, he concluded, and justly too, that the unequal distribution of temporal good was no evidence of partiality, it only argued the necessity and certainty of a future settlement; that the whole of life here, whether prosperous or otherwise, was only a state of trial, and at some time justice would be meted out to every one. In the experience of David we have a lively picture of the perplexity and disquietude of many honest and well-meaning persons. But if they would go and consult with God as he did, they would see, as he saw, that the felicity of the wicked is but of short duration, and will end in wretchedness at last. They would find also that the crosses, losses, and difficulties which seem to surround the righteous are temporary, and are made instruments in preparing them for a better life. Prosperity often casts a veil over divine realities, which affliction and disappointment tear asunder, and thus affording such views of future realities as could never otherwise be seen. Charnock says that "God often lays the sum of his amazing providences in very dismal afflictions, as the limner first puts on the dusky colors on which he intends to draw the portraiture of some illustrious beauty." Bishop Hall says that "every man has his turn of trouble and sorrow, whereby (some more, some less,) all men are in their times miserable. I never yet could meet with the man that complained not of somewhat." Punshon says, "Trial is God's glorious alchemistry, by which the dross is left in the crucible, the baser metals are transmuted, and the character is enriched with gold." Spurgeon says, "The very fact that you have troubles is a proof of his faithfulness; for you have got one half of his legacy, and you will have the other half. You know that Christ's last will and testament has two portions in it. 'In the world, ye shall have tribulation:' you have got that. The next clause is,

'In me ye shall have peace;' you have that too. 'Be of good cheer: I have overcome the world;' that is yours also." It is a beneficent arrangement of divine providence, that our disappointments, conflicts, and afflictions only tend to cultivate and develope virtues, which will survive when the wail of expiring time is heard.

> "And though sometimes thou seem'st thy face to hide,
>   As one that had withdrawn his love from me,
> 'Tis that my faith may to the full be tried,
>   And that I may thereby the better see
>   How weak I am, when not upheld by thee."

A workman was observed holding a half-polished pebble in a pair of iron pincers, and holding it against a rough stone. The stone whirled very rapidly; and when asked why he did it, he answered, "This is a diamond, and I want to grind off every flaw and crack in it. The fact is," said the workman, "this diamond, if it will bear the stone long enough, is to occupy an important place in the crown we are making up for our king. We have to grind and polish them a great while, but when they are done they are very beautiful." Ah! Christian, you must not be too hasty in impugning the mercy of God. This grinding and polishing, whilst it may be grievous and painful for the present, is only intended to prepare you for a place in the crown of the King of Glory. "See, father," said a boy, "they are knocking away the props from under the bridge. What are they doing that for? Won't it fall?" "They are knocking them away," said the father, "that the timbers may rest more firmly upon the stone piers, which are now finished." So God, by afflictions and trials, often knocks away the props upon which we have been unconsciously resting, that we may rest more firmly on Christ, who is the Rock of Ages.

All who are with an earnest purpose seeking for glory, honor, immortality, and eternal life must often feel, while under the influence of the world's chilling blast, a deep and abiding consolation in the simple belief that by and by full and complete justice will be rendered to every one. Justice and mercy are the two pillars of our great Mediator's throne. And although Christians are for a while compelled to walk in darkness, and receive cold and cruel treatment from the men of this world, yet there comes a time when all will receive their dues, that "the Judge of all the earth will do right."

In this "time haze," when we are compelled to look at everything through a glass darkly, it is not surprising if we should not be able to understand all the plans and purposes of the Almighty.

Why God permits or orders that some men be rich and others poor, some to be raised to honor and others to be dishonored, some to be loved and others to be hated, some to die in the flush of manhood and others to live out even more than the measure of human life, some to enjoy uninterrupted health and others to suffer for many long and weary years, we can not tell. One purpose may be to humble the pride of human reason. If men, by their own wisdom, could find out all the ways and plans of Providence; if they could penetrate into the future and tell all the events yet to come, as the astronomer can tell the time of an eclipse of the sun, they would become more self-willed and naughty than they now are. As it is, the proud philosopher and the beggar must sit side by side and wait the coming of events. Another purpose may be to draw us into closer communion with God, and to impress upon our minds the solemn truth that there is one above us. And still another purpose may be that a full and complete knowledge of all the plans of God, especially in relation to ourselves, is intended in the long annals of eternity to furnish a high degree of felicity to the saints. There is no reason to doubt but that the saved in heaven will be permitted to look back over life, and be made acquainted with any events which for the present are concealed in

They will then see and understand, as they can not now understand, the pains God took in leading them to heaven. They will see that these frequent changes, afflictions, losses, disappointments, and bereavements were all necessary, and that the hand of God was in every one of them. They will see and understand, as they can not now comprehend, that "justice and judgment are the habitation of his throne." That sainted mother, as she stands with her little one on the plains of light, will understand why it was taken away from her, during her pilgrimage through life.

> "The words of Heaven, on whom it will, it will;
> On whom it will not, so; yet still 'tis just."

Another source of consolation arising from a belief in the doctrine of providence, is the absolute veracity of God. "Let God be true, but every man a liar." Rom. iii. 4. God is true in and of himself. "Know therefore that the Lord thy God, he is God, the faithful God, which keepeth covenant mercy with them that love him and keep his commandments to a thousand generations." Deut. vii. 9. "My covenant will I not break, nor alter the thing that is gone out of my lips." Ps. lxxxix. 34. "In hope of eternal life, which God, that can not lie, promised before the world began." Tit. i. 2. "He is a God of truth." He truly and really exists; all his perfections and attributes are true and real. He is all he has represented himself to be. He is the eternal and only fountain of truth; being true in himself, all his works in creation, redemption, and providence are true and righteous altogether. He will faithfully perform everything he has said; not a jot or tittle will fail.

It is said that Lord Chatham was especially noted for his veracity, in making good whatever he had promised. At one time he promised that his son should be present and witness the pulling down of a certain garden wall. The wall, however, was taken down in the absence of his son, the father having forgotten his promise. When he remembered his promise, he felt the importance of fulfilling it, and immediately ordered his workmen to rebuild the wall, that his son might be present to witness its demolition. But our God never forgets, not even the least of his promises. What he has said that he will do. Clouds and darkness may surround his throne; worlds and systems may be created and set in motion; but if in the midst of these sublime acts an obscure Christian whispers in silent devotion, "Our Father which art in heaven," that whisper is heard, and the request noted.

In the early history of man God said to him, in

the fullness of time the seed of the woman should bruise the serpent's head. And it was so. Although four thousand years were occupied in the work of preparation, during which time many generations had come and gone, kingdoms had been founded, cities built and passed away, the promise survived all the changes and revolutions of forty centuries, and was fulfilled at last. It was said that the scepter should "not depart from Judah, nor a lawgiver from between his feet, until Shiloh come." And it was so. All that God, by the mouth of his prophets, said respecting the birth, suffering, death, and resurrection of Jesus Christ was fulfilled. God, in the person of his Son, said that Jerusalem with all its glory should pass away, and it did. Jesus, by divine authority, said that the Holy Ghost should come, and it came. If it were necessary, we could fill many pages with instances of the veracity of God. The Scriptures are the Scriptures of truth. Truth is as eternal as God himself—"Thy word is truth." Truth will never die; it can not die. If then God is truth in and of himself, it will survive the wreck of worlds. Latin says, "It takes a good many shovelfuls of earth to bury the truth." Swiss says, "Truth seldom goes without a scratched faith. Truth is God's daughter."

> "Marble and recording brass decay,
> And, like th' engraver's memory, pass away;
> The work of man inherit, as is just,
> Their author's frailty, and return to dust;
> But truth divine forever stands secure,
> Its head is guarded, as its base is sure;
> Fixed in the rolling flood of endless years,
> The pillar of the eternal plan appears;
> The raving storm and dashing wave defies,
> Built by the Architect who built the skies."

It has been declared by divine authority that "all things work together for good to them that love God." Rom. viii. 28. It is not said that all things work together for good to everybody, but to "them that love God." He has not told us how all things work together for good. He only says it is so, and God is not a man that he should lie. He has nowhere promised to show his beloved how all things are working, neither that any one thing was working independently of all the rest—all things work together. He did not say that all things should, or might, or ought to work together for good. All things work—are now working—together. In this "all things" are included the the workings of his Spirit and the operations of his providences,—all working together for good. "Whatever troubles, or afflictions, or disappointments, or persecutions may arise, God presses everything into the service; and they make a part of the general working, and are caused to contribute to the general good of that person who now loves God, and who is working by faith and love under the influence and operation of the Holy Ghost." "Oh, if I could see," says one, "how God is working; how he is turning this affliction, this sorrow, this disappointment, this bereavement, this persecution, and these reverses of fortune to my good, I would be satisfied. But my way is dark, very dark and gloomy; I can not see one step before me." Child of sorrow and disappointment, can you not trust all in the hands of your heavenly Father? Who that ever trusted in him was confounded? Who that ever leaned upon him for support fell? Who that ever sought in trouble that did not find him? Tell me, did God ever make a covenant and then fail to keep it? David said, "I have been young, and now am old: yet have I not seen the righteous forsaken, nor his seed begging bread." God is faithful, and will fulfill all his promises.

But our almost constant desire to see and understand precisely how God is working for us, what this is for, and what that means, gives us a vast amount of unnecessary trouble. If we would exercise more implicit confidence in the veracity of God, it would save us from a thousand distracting fears. But when his waves and billows are rolling over us, and we see nothing but thick dark clouds hanging about his throne, we grow faint, and anxiously cast about for a way to escape. We are always in a hurry to get away from afflictions, when in fact they may be just what we need. The apostle declares that we shall not be tempted above that we are able, but with the temptation there should be a way to escape. Now the veracity of God is pledged to keep this way to escape open; and to make it doubly sure, Jesus himself passed through all the temptations and left the way open, and all the powers of earth and hell can not close it up. Now this, with every other promise in the Bible, rests for its fulfillment upon the eternal veracity of God, and will as certainly be fulfilled as that God exists. If then, in the operations of divine providence, we are for a time under the influence of temptation, we should not complain, but trust in the promise of God. Luther says, "Once upon a time the devil came to me, and said, 'Martin Luther, you are a great sinner, and you will be damned.' Stop, stop. One thing at a time. I am a great sinner; that is true, though you have no right to tell me of it; I confess it. What next? Therefore you will be damned. That is not good reasoning. It is true I am a great sinner; but it is written, 'Jesus Christ came to save sinners,' therefore I shall be saved. So I cut the devil off with his own sword,

16

and he went away mourning, because he could not cast me down by calling me a sinner." In like manner, if we have the sword of the Spirit always in hand, we may defeat the adversary every time. For there is not a condition in which a good man can be placed where there is not also a promise to meet it.

No matter how dark and mysterious the leadings of divine providence may be, faith in God will bring quiet to the heart. Some years since, a vessel out at sea was overtaken by a terrible storm. The winds and waves were in violent commotion. The vessel seemed to be nothing more than a ball tossed about by their force. The passengers were greatly alarmed, expecting every moment to find a watery grave. In the midst of the storm the captain of the ship took hold of the helm. Shortly after, one of the passengers saw the captain's little boy sitting apparently with as much composure as if there was nothing more than an ordinary gale. He asked the boy if he was not afraid. "No, sir, I am not," was the prompt reply. "But why are you not afraid in such a terrible storm as this?" "My father is at the helm, sir, and everything is safe." Christian, can you not think of this? Can not you believe it? When the winds are whistling around you, and the angry waves are dashing against your vessel, and the thunders are crashing through the clouds over you, can not you remember that your Father is at the helm, and that all is safe as long as he is guiding the ship?

When Peter looked down at the waves, he began to sink. If he had kept his eyes on Jesus, he could have walked well enough. "Can you climb?" asked a captain of a sailor boy, before taking him out in his ship. "I can try," said the boy. Soon after the ship left the port the trial was made. The boy undertook to climb to the masthead, but began to grow dizzy as he mounted higher and higher on the rigging. "Oh! I shall fall," he said, as he looked down upon the sea. "Look up, look up, my boy," shouted the captain. And he did look up, and soon reached the masthead. Thus it is with us. When we look below and see the waves, we fear, or, like Peter, we begin to sink; but keep the eye fixed on Jesus,— "look up,"—and the difficulty is overcome. Let the storm-king rage if he will; let the lion roar if he must; let afflictions, persecutions, and sorrows come if they need be—"look up," and remember that He who can not lie has said, "I will never leave thee, nor forsake thee."

"Lord, I submit. Complete thy gracious will,
For, if thou slay me, I will trust thee still.
Oh, be my will so swallowed up in thine,
That I may do thy will, in doing mine.

CHAPTER XI.

CONSOLATION ARISING FROM A BELIEF IN THE DOCTRINE OF PROVIDENCE—CONTINUED. THE GOODNESS, SUFFICIENCY, LONG-SUFFERING, AND MERCY OF GOD.

> "Faith and hope
> Will teach me how to bear my lot;
> To think almighty wisdom best,
> To bow my head, and murmur not.
> The chast'ning hand of One above
> Falls heavy, but I kiss the rod;
> He gives the wound, and I must trust
> Its healing to the self-same God."

A firm, unyielding faith in God is absolutely necessary in order to derive consolation from a consideration of the attributes and perfections of the Almighty. Our faith in God must have that special characteristic by which we are able to trust everything in the hands of God, and believe that everything is working for good, whether we comprehend its workings or not. A Bible faith will hush our murmurings and complainings, and whisper in the ear of God, Father, it is well. Zwingli was a man of powerful faith, and expressed the very idea of trust in God that I desire to develope in this connection. He says,

"The blows by which people are endeavoring to subvert the house of God are so rude, and the assaults made upon it are so frequent, that it is not only the winds and rain that beat upon it, according to our Lord's prediction, but hail and lightning. Had I not perceived that the Lord was preserving the vessel, I should long ago have thrown the helm into the sea. I behold him through the tempest strengthening the cordage, adjusting the yards, spreading the sails, and commanding the very winds. Should I not, then, be a coward, unworthy the name of man, were I to abandon my post? I commit myself wholly to his sovereign goodness. Let him govern: let him hasten or delay; let him plunge us into the bottom of the abyss; we will fear nothing."

Faith in God is the great lever by which mountains are turned over, and trees are raised from their very roots. God is working, always working, and, to our beclouded vision, often working in mysterious ways; but faith says it is right, no matter how thick and threatening the clouds may be which surround the throne. God is in the midst of the darkness, and all is well, all is safe and secure. "Several German princes were once extolling the glory of their realms. One boasted of his excellent vineyards; another of his hunting grounds; another of his mines. At last, Abelard, Duke of Wurtemburg, took up the subject, and said, 'I own that I am a poor prince, and can vie with none of these things; nevertheless, I too possess a noble jewel in my dominion; for were I to be without attendants, either in the open country or wild forests, I could ask the first of my subjects whom I met to stretch himself upon the ground, and confidently place my head upon his bosom, and fall asleep without the slightest apprehension of injury.'" "Was not this," says Gotthold, "a precious jewel for a prince? I, however, have something better; for I can rest my head and heart in the lap of God's providence, and upon the bosom of Jesus Christ our Lord, with a perfect assurance that neither man nor devil can touch me there."

If God would permit us to see and understand all the workings of his providences, we could then get along tolerably well without faith; but the comforts growing out of trust would measurably be lost. I conceive that we are so constituted that we could not be happy without some one in whom to trust, and upon whom to rely. God, in the order of divine providence, has so arranged the affairs in the kingdom of nature, as well as in the kingdom of grace, that faith is an absolute necessity. I conceive that the happiness of all intelligent beings, whether in heaven or on the earth, to some extent depends upon their faith; and hence the notion that faith in the saint will die when he dies can not be true. If this were true, then the inhabitants of heaven must all be infidels, for I know of no state or condition between belief and unbelief. I know that with our obscure vision, it is often very difficult for us to harmonize the dispensations of God's providence even with his goodness. We know that God is infinitely and eternally good; but there are so many strange and mysterious things transpiring around us, that seem to be so utterly at variance with our abstract notions of goodness, that we are often utterly bewildered. By the force of circumstances, over which we have no control, we are driven this way and that way, contrary to all our preferences, that we wonder how a good God could permit it.

But the goodness of God is, nevertheless, very clearly and beautifully set forth in the Holy Scriptures. God is infinitely, immutably, and eternally good. And whatever he does in heaven or on the earth, is and must be in harmony with this perfection of his nature. You that have been led over rough and rugged ways, until your hearts were sore and feet bleeding, hear the word of the Lord. "O give thanks unto the Lord; for he is good; his mercy endureth forever." I. Chron. xvi. 34. "O taste and see that the Lord is good: blessed is the man that trusteth in him." Ps. xxxiv. 8. "They shall abundantly utter the memory of thy great goodness, and shall sing of thy righteousness." Ps. cxlv. 7. "The Lord is good to all: and his tender mercies are over all his works." Ps. cxlv. 9.

From these passages it is not difficult to believe, if we believe the Scriptures at all, that God is good; but how to harmonize this perfection of his nature with the operations of his providence we are not always able to perceive. Wicked men, who are the avowed enemies of God and his cause on earth, are often apparently more happy than the righteous; they are often prospered in temporal matters, and have all that heart could wish; whilst, on the other hand, the most pious and devoted Christians are often very poor and afflicted. "If we look at all the retinue of believers, following Christ up the steep ascent, we behold them bearing the cross, while the rugged path is marked by the blood of their feet, and their eyes are wet with weeping. They come out of great tribulation." Not so with the ungodly. They often build for themselves fine houses, and gather about them the light and gay, and with singing and dancing, go merrily through life.

Now if God is infinitely and eternally good, why does he permit this great difference?

God has various ways of manifesting his goodness. "The rainbow that is about the throne may have its distinguishable colors, but the ray is one, and its name is love." "For thou, Lord, art good, and ready to forgive; and plenteous in mercy unto all them that call upon thee. * * * A God full of compassion, and gracious, long-suffering, and plenteous in mercy and truth." Ps. lxxxvi. 5, 15. If God had intended that all men should be fully rewarded and fully punished in this life, it would be very difficult to harmonize his goodness with the operations of his providence; but there is another world, another time and place of reckoning. God often permits even the worst of men to prosper, and his children to be poor and afflicted. When Lazarus was in heaven and Dives in torments, Abraham said to the rich man, "Son, remember that thou in thy life-time receivedst thy good things, and likewise Lazarus evil things: but now he is comforted, and and thou art tormented." Luke xvi. 25. So God often suffers it to be. But in all the poverty, afflictions, persecutions, and distresses of his loved ones, his eye of pity and compassion is upon them. If a stranger had passed by the gate of the rich man where Lazarus lay, he might have said: "Poor, forsaken man, how sad his condition must be." He would not likely have seen the angels that were in waiting to carry him away to the better land. Judging from a human standpoint, the condition of the rich man was more to be desired than that of afflicted Lazarus. Thus in the hurry and bustle of life we are too apt to judge from outside appearances, forgetting that God is on the inside, working all things after the counsel of his own will. In the prophet's vision of the mystic wheels (Ezekiel i. 1), he saw above it all the appearance of a throne, and the appearance of a man on the throne; then there was also the "appearance of the bow." Now in this we are clearly taught that everything is governed by one power, one ruler, for there was but one throne, and one man on the throne. The appearance of the bow was the sign of God's covenant of mercy and goodness. The cloud which surrounds the throne may be fraught with thunder and flashing with lightnings, but there stands out in clear view the appearance of the bow—the covenant of grace.

God in his infinite goodness has provided a refuge for all, to which they may fly in the day of trouble. "Walk about Zion, and go round about her: tell the towers thereof. Mark ye well her bulwarks, consider her palaces; that ye may tell it to the generation following. For this God is our God forever and ever: he will be our guide even unto death." Ps. xlviii. 12–14. "God is known in her palaces for a refuge." When the water-floods rage, and all above and around is in wild and fearful consternation, the Christian, however poor he may be, persecuted and forsaken of men as was Lazarus, may hear the voice of his Father in heaven calling him: "Come, my people, enter thou into thy chambers, and shut thy doors about thee: hide thyself as it were for a little moment, until the indignation be overpast." Is. xxvi. 20. The good man, while the storm rages without, may, nevertheless, boldly say: "God is our refuge and strength, a very present help in trouble. Therefore will we not fear, though the earth be removed, and though the mountains be carried into the midst of the sea; though the waters thereof roar and be troubled, though the mountains shake with the swelling thereof." An excellent writer has said, "Our refuges are like the nests of birds; in summer they are hidden among the leaves, but in winter they are seen among the naked branches." A German, soon after his conversion, was overheard in secret prayer to say: "O Lord Jesus, I didn't know you were so good." A Sunday-school teacher had upon the blackboard the sentence, "The Lord is good to all," and requested his class to repeat it. One little boy refused, because he said it is not true. "God is not good to father and me. He has taken my little brother away; and father is at home crying about it." The teacher explained to the little boy how God in his goodness had taken him away; that if he had been permitted to remain with them, he might have suffered in many ways; that God was a good shepherd, and sometimes took the tender lambs away from the cold winter of life; that his little brother was not lost, but was safe with the angels in heaven, and that by and by the Lord Jesus would take him and his father up to dwell with his little brother; but they must be good and patient. "Oh!" said the child, with evident emotion, "I'll go and tell father." He did so; and with these higher views of the goodness of God their hearts were comforted, and they were content. Many a sad and sorrowing heart would be consoled under bereavements did they understand the designs of God. And here faith comes in as a substitute for knowledge. If we do not and can not understand the designs of God, we should trust him, for he is wise and good.

God is no respecter of persons, but is good to all, and seeks to promote the highest interest of all. But this perfection of his nature can only operate in harmony with every other perfection of his nature. God loves all, but he is especially good to those that are good. He feeds and favors all, but reveals himself to his children as he does not to his enemies. Jesus said, "He that loveth me shall be loved of my Father, and I will love him, and will manifest myself to him." John xiv. 21. It is the privilege of all to share in these special manifestations of God's goodness and love. It is true that God often leads his beloved by paths they had not known, yet in all this his goodness is especially concerned. "The goodness of God can not be manifested more clearly than in a sanctifying process. Again and again we have besought the Lord to withdraw us from evil ways, to divorce us from the rivals which seduce; and now we hear him saying, 'I will hedge up thy way with thorns, and make a wall, that she shall not find her paths. * * * Then shall she say, I will go and return to my first husband; for then was it better with me than now.' And so saying, the soul recognizes the goodness of God, and by faith enters the stronghold. There are thoughts in the darkened chamber of sorrow which visit us nowhere else,—important, salutary thoughts, to instruct, confirm, purify, arm, and comfort; thoughts of our sin, our selfishness, our idolatry, our unbelief; thoughts of the abiding joy laid up in heaven, where sickness, alarm, despair, and sin never come. And I speak the mind of all sanctified affliction when I add that, among them all, no thought is more constant than that of God's goodness as an eternal refuge."

> "God hath created nights
> As well as days to deck the varied globe;
> Grace comes as oft clad in the dusky robe
> Of desolation, as in white attire."

Christians should not lose sight of the goodness of God, nor for a moment imagine that he is angry with them, when he seems to withdraw from them. Does a father necessarily cease to be good when he corrects his child? If God would permit us at all times to have our own way, we would go directly to ruin. It is the goodness of God that moves him to turn our course. "He doth not afflict willingly." "As a father pitieth his child, so the Lord pitieth them that fear him." God would shine on us all the time if it were best for us. If it were not for our self-reliance, forgetfulness, and want of faith, he would cause us to fly to his bosom. But we are haughty, stubborn, and self-willed, and hence must be corrected and subdued. We must feel our worthlessness, our weakness, and our dependence, else we would never look up for divine help. Jesus said, "I will that they also, whom thou hast given me, be with me where I am; that they may behold my glory." Now in order that we may be with Christ, in the place that he said he would go to prepare, we must not only have a title to it, but a fitness for it; and God is doing all he can, consistent with the principles of a perfectly righteous, moral government, to bring us to the inheritance of his beloved Son. Afflictions, sorrows, tribulations, disappointments, persecutions, losses, bereavements, and crosses, are all necessary, under the supervision of a wise and benevolent Providence, to work in us the necessary preparation for that higher, holier, and better state.

"Heaven but tries our virtues by affliction,
And oft the cloud which wraps the present hour
Serves but to brighten all our future days."

Another source of consolation, in the midst of dark and inexplicable providences, is the all-sufficiency of God. For a Christian to know and feel that under every possible and conceivable circumstance in which he may or can be placed, that there is in God whatever he may or can need, is a consolation, for the sake of which a monarch might be willing to lay down his crown. God is an all-sufficient being, and does not need creation in general, nor men and angels in particular. Neither can the services of men or angels add anything to his perfections. He is not worshiped with men's hands, as though he needed anything. "Can a man be profitable unto God, as he that is wise may be profitable unto himself? Is it any pleasure to the Almighty, that thou art righteous? or is it gain to him, that thou makest thy ways perfect?" Job xxii. 2, 3. God is all-sufficient in himself, because he has at his command enough to give all his creatures. If it were necessary, he could create millions of worlds and systems to supply the wants of his creatures. The earth, and all its fullness, is his; the heaven of heavens is his; time and eternity are his. He is the fullness and perfection of power, wisdom, justice, benevolence, and mercy. Nothing can be added nor taken away. He is all—I AM. He is the giver of all life, and is able to support and sustain all things. He is all-sufficient in the kingdom of grace. No matter where his people are, nor what their surroundings may be, he is able to sustain and uphold them. Are you thirsty? He can bring water from the rock. Are you hungry? He can cover the ground with manna. By his all-sufficient grace he could sustain the martyrs—yea, all that will trust in him. "Do they cast us out of the city?" asked Gregory Nazianzen. "They can not cast us out of that which is in heaven. If they who hate us could do this, they would be doing something real against us. So long, however, as they can not do this, they are but pelting us with drops of water, or striking us with the wind." It is related of a Gallic lord that as he was led forth to martyrdom, he discovered that out of regard to his rank the officers put no chains on him, such as his brethren which were being led forth wore. Upon seeing this he said: "Let me, I pray you, be clipped of none of my honors; I too, for love to Jesus, would wear a chain." Christian, God is abundantly able to bear you up through any and all of your trials.

> "When persecution's torrent blaze
>   Wraps the unshrinking martyr's head,
> When fade all earthly flowers and lays,
>   When summer friends are gone and fled,
> Is he alone in that dark hour,
> Who owns the Lord of love and power?
>
> Or moves there not around their brow,
>   A wand no human arm may wield,
> Fraught with a spell no angels know,
>   His steps to guide, his soul to shield?
> Thou, Savior, art his charmed bower,
> His magic ring, his rock, his tower."

Saints in ages past believed this blessed and soul-inspiring doctrine. They felt their own insufficiency, and did not arrogate to themselves the power to stand alone. Paul said, "Not that we are sufficient of ourselves to think anything as of ourselves; but our sufficiency is of God." II. Cor. iii.

5. **Paul felt that he was nothing of** himself, but on account of the communicable sufficiency of Christ he could do all things that were necessary. When he was under severe trial he besought the Lord to relieve him of it. But the thorn was not removed; nevertheless, God did for him what was infinitely better, for he said, "my grace is sufficient." Paul was better off with the thorn, and the grace to bear it, than he would have been if the thorn had been taken away. So we in our afflictions, trials, and conflicts, if we have grace to bear them, are always the better for having gone through them. Every victory gained only prepares for another and greater victory. Daniel was none the worse for having spent a night in the lion's den. The three Hebrews were in every respect the better for having gone through the fire, especially since it is that the smell of fire was not on their garments. Christian, if it were not necessary for you to be afflicted God would not permit it to come upon you. A good man when asked how he could bear his afflictions so patiently, answered, "It lightens the stroke to draw near to him that handles the rod." God would have us near to him. hence sometimes uses the rod for this purpose. S. Coley says that "fire and hammer and file are necessary to give the metal form; and it must have many a grind and many a rub ere it will

shine; so in trial, character is shaped and beautified and brightened." Then let trials and afflictions come if need be, God is all-sufficient, and is abundantly able, and correspondingly willing, to communicate to his beloved the necessary grace and strength to bear them up. "I would gladly take your tract," said a soldier as he lay in a hospital, "but I have lost both my arms in battle; and I would gladly lose them again, were it possible, rather than not enjoy what I now possess. While I was far away in the woods, and did not know I should ever get back to camp, I cried unto the Lord in good earnest, and he had mercy on my soul."

> "A life all ease is all abused;—
> O precious grace! that made thee wise
> To know—affliction rightly used
> Is mercy in disguise."

The long-suffering of God is a source of great consolation to a thoughtful Christian. What would become of us if God were not patient and forbearing? If he had dealt with us according to the manner and magnitude of our offenses, we would have perished long ago. And even since we have professed faith in the Lord Jesus Christ, nothing but the long-suffering of God has saved us. We have often murmured and complained and even found fault with the providences of God. In our blindness and disquietude we have often reached out our hand, and felt for the helm, proposing to guide the vessel ourselves. More than half the time we have signified in one way and another that we were displeased with the dispensations of God's providences. This is not right, and that is wrong. It is too warm or cold, or wet or dry. We are not what nor where we want to be. Our want of patience has been and still is offensive to God. "O impatient ones! Did the leaves say nothing to you as they murmured when you came hither to-day? They were not created this spring, but months ago: and the summer just begun will fashion others for another year. At the bottom of every leaf-stem is a cradle, and in it is an infant germ; and the winds will rock it, and the birds will sing to it all summer long; and next season it will unfold. So God is working for you, and carrying forward to the perfect development all the processes of your lives." Many of us are somewhat like the farmer who wanted rain for his grass and sunshine for his wheat all at the same time. We are full of murmuring and complaining. T. Brooks, in speaking of the evil of murmuring, says, "It is a sin that breeds many other sins, namely, disobedience, contempt, ingratitude, impatience, distrust, rebellion, cursing, carnality; yea, it charges God with folly, yea, with blasphemy. The language of a murmuring soul is this: 'Surely God might have done this sooner, and that wiser, and the other thing better.'" Now I would not be uncharitable, nor bring a railing accusation against Christians, yet I fear that the majority of us, one time and another, have been guilty of such offenses as those named above. What then would become of us, if we had not a long-suffering and patient Father?

There are many instances of the long-suffering and patience of God recorded in the Holy Scriptures. How long he waited in the days of Noah. How long he bore with the murmurings and complainings of the children of Israel,—"Forty years long was I grieved with this generation." The Savior furnishes a most beautiful and instructive illustration of the long-suffering and patience of God in the parable of the barren fig-tree: "These three years I come seeking fruit on this fig-tree, and find none." In this manner God waits and watches for fruit; and in like manner he bears with our murmurings and disquietudes. "Oh, the omnipotent patience of God."

"In patience, then, possess thy soul,
Stand still! for while the thunders roll,

> Thy Savior sees thee through the gloom,
> And will to thy assistance come;
> His love and mercy will be shown
> To those who trust in him alone."

A few passages of scripture will, perhaps, assist us in forming higher views of the long-sufferings of God. "And the Lord passed by before him, and proclaimed, The Lord, The Lord God, merciful and gracious, long-suffering, and abundant in goodness and truth, keeping mercy for thousands, forgiving iniquity and transgression and sin." Ex. xxxiv. 6, 7. "But thou, O Lord, art a God full of compassion, and gracious, long-suffering, and plenteous in mercy and truth." Ps. lxxxvi. 15. In prosperity and adversity, in sickness and in health, in the light or in the darkness, at home or abroad, among friends or among foes, everywhere, and under all circumstances, we should remember the blessed, soul-inspiring truth that "God is full of compassion, and gracious, long-suffering, and plenteous in mercy and truth."

Christians in their best estate are but feeble worms of the dust. They have nothing of which they can boast. Sin has weakened and enfeebled the whole man. He is a wreck. But Jesus said, "A bruised reed shall he not break, and smoking flax shall he not quench." The reed at best is but an insignificant growth among the trees of the forest. But mark the language: it is not a sound, healthy reed, but one that has been crushed,—a bruised reed; one that in itself is altogether worthless. The moral lesson taught in this passage is the gracious compassion and long-suffering of the Almighty. Sin has so bruised and crippled us, that we are like a bruised reed and smoking flax. One said, when he had well considered his worthlessness, "I am but a rush, a reed, a bruised reed; of little value to my neighbor; of no value to my God. I am feeble in knowledge. There is more in Scripture that is dark than light to my understanding. I am in doubt and perplexity. * * * I am weak in purpose, and failing in resolution; weak in conflict, and often flying before my enemies." Now what would become of such a Christian if God were not long-suffering, patient, and kind? But God, blessed be his name for evermore, knows all about our weaknesses, and in the order of his divine providence has made ample provision for us. He tempers the cold wind to the shorn lamb, and when it is too weak to walk will bear it in his bosom, close to his great warm heart. If God did not provide the means and the way for our escape, and then help us along, we would very soon be overtaken and crushed.

> 'O, shame upon thee, listless heart,
> So sad a sigh to heave,
> As if thy Savior had no part
> In thoughts that make thee grieve."

Another source of consolation to a Christian is the mercy of God. Among the numerous insults offered to God, I doubt if any is of greater magnitude than ingratitude. Ausanius says, "Nothing more detestable does the earth produce than an ungrateful man." Dr. South, in describing this character, says: "The ungrateful person is a monster which is all throat and belly,—a kind of thoroughfare, or common sewer for the good things of the world to pass into; and of whom, in respect of all kindness conferred on him, may be verified that observation of the lion's den, before which appeared the footsteps of many that had gone in thither, but no prints of any that ever came out thence." Whoever feels that he is without sin in this respect, let him cast a stone at his ungrateful neighbor. God, in the order of his good providences, has so arranged the affairs in the universe that man, fallen as he is, is made the receiver of numerous blessings, both spiritual and temporal; and in return he sends up to heaven murmurings and complainings. If the giver of every good and perfect gift were not a God of boundless mercy, the whole race of man would go quickly down to hell.

> "Though Nature her inverted course forego,
> The day forget to rest, the time to flow,
> Yet shall Jehovah's servant stand secure,
> His Mercy fixed, eternal shall endure;
> On them her everlasting rays shall shine,
> More mild and bright, and sure, O sun! than thine.'

"Mercy," says Dr. Gill, "differs in some respects both from the love and grace of God; from the love of God in its object and order of operation; mercy surpasses its objects, miserable and fallen; love seems to work by mercy, and mercy from it. All mercy is grace, yet all grace is not mercy." Dr. Spencer illustrates mercy on this wise: "A merchant, that keeps a book of debt and credit, writes both what is owing him and what he oweth himself, and then casteth up the whole. But God doth not so—his mercy is triumphant over his justice; and therefore wipes out what we owe him, and writes down only that which he owes us by promise." Some one said to Thomas Hooker, when he was dying: "You are going to receive the reward of your labor." "I am," said he, "going to receive mercy." John Bunyan said, "It must be great mercy, or no mercy; for little mercy will never serve my turn." Spurgeon says that it is "free as the air which belts the earth, and penetrates the peasant's cottage as well as the royal palace, without purchase or premium, so free is the mercy of God in Christ. It tarrieth not for thee as thou art. It waylayeth thee in love, it meets thee in tenderness."

Mercy is essential to the perfection of God, and is infinite, eternal, and common to all. It is great and abundant, as the word of God most directly teaches. "The Lord thy God is a merciful God; he will not forsake thee, neither destroy thee." Deut. iv. 31. "Nevertheless for thy great mercies' sake thou didst not utterly consume them, nor forsake them; for thou art a gracious and merciful God." Neh. ix. 31.

The mercy of God, in its exercise toward man, is his disposition not only to pardon sin, but also to succor those that are in distress. When we consider man in his fallen state,—corrupt, rebellious, and hateful in his behavior,—how vast, how amazingly great is that mercy that could be extended to him so freely. Old Testament saints were wont to recount the displays of divine mercy in the most glowing language. In Psalm cxxxvi. the author uses the language, "for the mercy of the Lord endureth forever," twenty-six times. It is the burden of every verse, and expresses the psalmist's view of the mercy of God in the past, and reaching far out into the future. The mercy of God was abundantly displayed in creation, in so wisely and benevolently arranging everything, so that the wants of all his creatures are amply provided for. His mercy was displayed in redemption. Sin made a ghastly wound, but the plaster which mercy provided is as wide and long as the wound. The mercy of God has been exhibited in his dealings with his people in all time past. And the Christian of to-day may, if he will, sit down and recount the mercy of God to him.

> "Mercy descends
> From heaven, and o'er the penitential heart,
> Rent by the agonizing pangs of guilt,
> Spreads the soft blessings of eternal peace."

Let the believer remember, in all the deep and inexpressible troubles of his soul, that God, by his omnipresence, is everywhere, and everywhere merciful. In trouble, in affliction, and in all manner of distresses, the justice, goodness, wisdom, benevolence, long-suffering, and mercy of God, like ministering angels, are around thee. If the way in which you are compelled to walk is strange, and even dark, mercy the while is with thee, for it endureth forever. Oh, if Christians could but comprehend the hight and depth and length and breadth of the mercy of God, they would cease to murmur and complain about their trials and conflicts. If they could believe that it was the hand of Mercy that led them into those thorny ways, they would rejoice rather than complain. God in his mercy often directs or permits his dearly beloved ones to be led over rugged mountains, and through dark ravines, that he may thereby deliver them from snares and pit-falls, into which they would have fallen if they had not been turned aside. Weary, tempted, and sorrowful one, can you believe this precious declaration of the word of God? "All the paths of the Lord are mercy and truth unto such as keep his covenant and his testimonies." Ps. xxv. 10. As long as a Christian continues to walk in the ways of God's commandments, he will be in the paths of mercy and truth. No matter how rough nor how uninviting the way may be, if it is God's way; it is mercy and truth. "God's mercy," says Spurgeon, "is so great, that it forgives great sins, to great sinners, after great lengths of time, and then gives great favors and great privileges, and raises us up to great enjoyments in the great heaven of the great God." Tempted, tired one, this great mercy is all on your side.

> "Why, all the souls that were, were forfeit once;
> And He that might the vantage best have took,
> Found out the remedy. How would you be,
> If He, which is the top of judgment, should
> But judge you as you are? Oh, think on that!
> And mercy then will breathe within your lips,
> Like man new made."

CHAPTER XII.

CONSOLATION DERIVED FROM A BELIEF IN THE DOCTRINE OF PROVIDENCE—CONTINUED. LOVE, AFFLICTIONS, AND CHASTISEMENTS.

"Before the sparkling lamp on high
Were kindled up, and hung around the sky;
Before the sun led on the circling hours,
Or vital seeds produced their active powers;
Before the first intelligences strung
Their golden harps, and soft preludiums sung
To Love, the mighty cause whence their existence sprung,
  Th' ineffable Divinity
  His own resemblance meets in thee.
By this, thy glorious lineage, thou dost prove
Thy high descent, for God himself is love."

"Whom the Lord loveth he chasteneth, and scourgeth every son whom he receiveth." Heb. xii. 6. God's love toward his children is in no way more clearly manifest than when he chasteneth them. It is a standing proof of his fatherly love, and shows his most gracious designs toward them. It were far better for a Christian that he should feel the rod every day, and every hour in the day, than that God should let him alone. "Whom the Lord loveth he chasteneth." And all who endure chastening, God dealeth with them as with sons; for what son is he whom the father chasteneth not? All who are without chastisement are bastards, and not sons. Heb. xii. 6–8.

That we may better understand how the love of God may be exhibited in chastisement, and how we may derive comfort and consolation therefrom, it will be necessary, in the first place, to consider something of the nature and extent of this love. "He that loveth not, knoweth not God; for God is love. * * * And we have known and believed the love that God hath to us. God is love; and he that dwelleth in love dwelleth in God, and God in him." I. John iv. 8, 16. God does not possess the passion of love as men do. It is not a mere impulse begotten from some cause independent of himself. It is his very nature; without it he would not be God. And in whatever way it may be exhibited to mortals, it shows his benevolent designs and purposes.

The love of God especially appears in the gift of his Son. "God so loved the world, that he gave his only begotten Son, that whosoever believeth in him should not perish, but have everlasting life." John iii. 16. "History's noblest deed and record of love was in the self-devotion of one generous heathen, Pylades, who forfeited his life to save *his friend;* but 'God commendeth his love to us, in that, while we were yet sinners,

Christ died for us.'" "You have not yet seen the greatest gift of all—the heart of God, the love of his heart. And will he in very deed show us that? Yes; unveil that cross, and see. It was his only mode of showing us his heart. It is infinite love laboring to reveal itself,—agonizing to utter the fullness of infinite love. Apart from that act, a boundless ocean of love would have remained forever shut up and concealed in the heart of God. But now it has found an ocean-channel. Beyond this he can not go. Once and forever the proof has been given,—'God is love.'"

The properties of this love, as developed in the word of God, are, 1. Everlasting. "The Lord hath appeared of old unto me, saying, Yea, I have loved thee with an everlasting love: therefore with loving-kindness have I drawn thee." Jer. xxxi. 3. 2. This love is declared to be immutable. "For I am the Lord, I change not; therefore ye sons of Jacob are not consumed." Mal. iii. 6. 3. It is free,—not the result of Christ's death, nor of man's merit, "for God so loved the world. that he gave his only begotten Son." The love of God is great and unspeakable. "God, who is rich in mercy, for his great love wherewith he loved us." Eph. ii. 4. "And to know the love of Christ, which passeth knowledge, that ye might be filled with all the fullness of God." Eph. iii. 19. Of the nature of this love, Mr. Rutherford says: "I can but wonder at three things in the love of Christ. First, freedom. Oh, that lumps of sin should get such love for nothing! Secondly, the sweetness of this love. I give over to speak or write of it; but those that feel it may better witness what it is: but it is so sweet, that, next to Christ himself, nothing can match it. Nay, I think that a soul could live eternally blessed on Christ's love, and feed upon no other thing. Thirdly, what power and strength are in this love! I am persuaded it can climb a steep hill with hell upon its back; and swim through water, and not drown; and sing in the fire, and find no pain; and triumph in losses, prisons, sorrow, exile, disgrace, and laugh and rejoice in death."

"God is love," and is therefore no respecter of persons. He loves all with the love of benevolence, and seeks to produce the highest possible good of mankind. Every flower that opens, every spire of grass that grows, every leaf that clings to its tiny branch, every bird that sings among the trees, with every living thing, may look up and say, "It is my sun that shines in the heavens." So every man, whether rich or poor, high or low, young or old, may look up and say, "God is my Father." Nevertheless, his love toward his children is manifested in a peculiar degree, because they have complied with his conditions, by which they have been brought into such harmony with his law, and communion with himself, that they can enjoy his love in a degree unknown to the carnal heart. "The love of God," says the apostle, "is shed abroad in our hearts, by the Holy Ghost which he has given unto us." All are most kindly and pressingly invited to come and participate in this fullness of love; but, alas! many will not come. All may love him, and enjoy those special communications of his love. He has provided a shelter for all; but the majority prefer to remain without, and meet the terrible storm that must shortly come upon them. He offers life to all; but a vast number prefer to die. Through the impulses of his eternal love he has made the most ample provision to save all men from sin on earth, and to save them eternally in heaven. If men are lost, it will not be because God did not love them, but because they would not love him.

"All things that are on earth shall wholly pass away,
Except the love of God, which shall live and last for aye."

Having then the assurance that God is love; that he loves all mankind with a love of benevolence, and especially manifests his love to such as love him; also, that whatever he does, however dark and mysterious it may appear to us at the time, is prompted by eternal love, the Christian can well afford to trust everything, for time and eternity, in his hands. If God is love, and if we love him, then whatever he does for us, with us, through us, or by us, must be intended for our highest good. Temporary afflictions may, and indeed often do, break with terrible fury over the heads of those who are most devoted to God; dark and gloomy days of adversity overtake them; their paths become exceedingly rough and mountainous. At such times let the soul turn to him that dwelleth in Zion; to him whose very nature is love, and find a warm and throbbing heart. Let the good man remember that all these afflictions, be their nature what they may, are ordered or permitted by a loving Father, and will be so controlled and overruled that they will end in his favor. Here and there, in tracing the lines of profane history, we may find a few shadowy outlines of heroic love: a mother died for her child, a husband perished for his wife; but when and where did a man die for his enemies? What king, or emperor, or ruler, watched with a father's pity and love over all his subjects? It is nowhere to be found in the history of man, but we find it in the history of God's dealings with a lost race.

While it is not said in the word of God that Christians are to be exempt from suffering, it is included in the promises that they shall be sustained and upheld. "When thou passest through the waters, I will be with thee; and through the rivers, they shall not overflow thee: when thou walkest through the fire, thou shalt not be burned; neither shall the flame kindle upon thee. For I am the Lord thy God, the Holy One of Israel, thy Savior." Is. xliii. 2, 3. And we are altogether safe when we assert that all a Christian will be required to suffer and endure, while in the way of his duties, is in some way necessary, and will turn to his advantage. A God of love will not permit those that love him to go to war at their own expense, neither will he permit them to suffer and be the losers. One thing often perplexes the minds of even good men, and that is, that they meet with trials and afflictions while striving to obey the commands of God. Jesus said to his disciples that they should cross over a certain water; and it was not until after they had left the shore that the storm came upon them. They were in the direct line of duty. But see! just at the right time Jesus came to their relief, and the disciples were all the better for having passed through the storm. So when difficulties overtake Christians while in the line of their duty, God, by his ever-working providence, will turn everything to their good in the end.

"When God visits us in affliction, it is as a man when he goes to try a vessel to see whether there be wine or water in it, and of what quality." In a journal of Rev. C. Simeon, of Cambridge, Scotland, I find the following entry: "Went to see Lady Ross's ground. There also I saw blind men weaving. One blind man being interrogated with respect to his knowledge of spiritual things, answered, 'I never saw till I was blind; nor did I ever know contentment when I had my eye-sight, as I do now that I have lost it; I can truly affirm, though few know how to credit me, that I would on no account change my present situation and circumstances with any I ever enjoyed before I was blind." When Henry Martin was near his end he said, "Why should I murmur? Weakness, peril, and pain are but ministering angels, whose office it is to conduct me to glory."

> "Each care, each ill of mortal birth,
> Is sent in pitying love,
> To lift the lingering heart from earth,
> And speed its flight above.

> And every pang that wrings the heart,
> And every joy that dies,
> Tell us to seek a purer rest,
> And trust to holier ties."

We can not tell the uses of affliction. We may not see anything but suffering in it. We see the beginning, but the end is hid from us. We judge only from what we see and feel. Who can tell how much dross there is about him, or how hot it would be necessary to make the furnace in order to separate the dross from the metal? Copper is first laid in aqua fortis before being engraved upon. So God often prepares us by afflictions, in order that he may make the more lasting impressions upon our minds. The inhabitants of heaven are all pure—"the pure in heart shall see God." God would purify every one of us, and for that purpose often allows the furnace to be made very hot. Bishop Hall said: "We beat back the flame not with the purpose to suppress it, but to raise it higher and diffuse it more. These afflictions and repulses, which seem to be discouragements, are indeed the merciful incidents of grace. If God did mean judgment to my soul, he would either withdraw the fuel, or pour water upon the fire, or suffer it to languish for want of motives; but now that he continues to me the means, and opportunities, and desires of good, I shall misconstrue the intention of my God, if I shall think his crosses sent rather to damp than to quicken his Spirit in me."

But we must have faith in the doctrine of a universal providence. We must believe that the goodness, mercy, benevolence, wisdom, and love of God are all immediately connected with his operations, otherwise we will constantly be liable to misinterpret his designs, and thereby measurably rob ourselves of the intended benefits. "Oh," says that discouraged Christian, "I could endure these misfortunes if I could see any providence in it." Many there are who bear up under their afflictions with a kind of stoic indifference, because they believe it just happened so, or was brought about by some caprice of chance. Now, while it is true that we may have been the instruments of bringing the misfortune upon us, we are not to suppose that God takes no notice of it, or that he is or can be indifferent about the results of it. God can use any instrumentality he chooses to correct an existing wrong, or prevent a greater calamity. Because we may be the instruments of our own troubles, does not preclude the operations of divine providence, no more than though God would use any other instrumentality. Jonah was the chief instrument in bringing himself into difficulty, but God was present and controlled all the circumstances, and at last helped him out of his trouble. The truth is, that "under the equitable Master whom we serve we do not suffer a single affliction that hath not for its foundation either his justice, which corrects us for our sins, or his mercy, which would prevent the faults into which we are liable to fall. There is not one affliction, therefore, which is not either just chastisement or a merciful preservation."

To cause a barren tree to bear fruit, it is sometimes necessary to dig about it and enrich the soil; in other cases it is necessary to cut the stock and lopp off the useless branches. When Mr. Cecil was walking in the Botanical Garden of Oxford, he saw a pomegranate tree that was cut almost through the stem. He asked the gardener why he did it. He replied, "Sir, this tree used to shoot so strong that it bore nothing but leaves; I was therefore obliged to cut it in this manner; and when it was almost cut through then it began to bear plenty of fruit." So God, in his wise and good providences, is often compelled to trim his trees, and sometimes to cut them almost through. But whether he digs about them and enriches the soil, or uses the knife, it is all for the same purpose—to make more fruitful. Meantime all the digging, cutting, and pruning is prompted by the love of God. If he did not love us he would let us alone. It was love that moved the great heart of God to give his Son to die for a lost and ruined world. God does not afflict willingly. He permits it, because it is necessary. If it were not for our waywardness, if we were not so unbelieving, if we were not so forgetful, he would let his sun shine on us all the time. There are very few Christians, if indeed there are any, that could stand continued prosperity. Paul had been favored above many of his fellow Christians, and lest, as he says himself, he should become exalted above measure, there was given him a thorn in the flesh. This was a preventive. So God often deals with his loved ones, to save them from ruin.

There is a vast difference between what we need and what we want. If God would give us all we want, it would ruin us. In his love he gives us what we need. As a rule, we all want prosperity, health, friends, and riches. Now if these things were best for us, God would certainly give them to us; but it is just as much like a loving and benevolent Father to withhold them if he sees they will harm us. It would please a child to give it a looking-glass and a hammer; but what parent, no matter how dearly he loves his child, would gratify its wish. As Christians, we are not apt to ask God to afflict us, or to put us into the furnace, and yet this may be the very thing we most need. There may be a great deal of dross about us that must be removed, and nothing but a hot furnace will do it. We ask for a blessing, and God answers by fire—not as we would have dictated, however. God gives us just what we need. "A furnace," says Mr. B. Keach, "refines gold, and makes it much purer than before; so afflictions refine and make more holy. 'When he hath tried me, I shall come forth as gold.' A furnace is sometimes made very hot. according to the kind and condition of the metal: so are afflictions sometimes very grievous, heavy, and trying, as the case may require. A furnace will destroy tin, lead, etc., and also the drossy part of gold; so affliction burns up the loose and hypocritical, and purges them from all their corruption. The metal, when it comes forth from the furnace, is more prepared for its proper use; so are the people of God when they come forth from affliction."

Jeremiah said. "He doth not afflict willingly, nor grieve the children of men." Lam. iii. 33. God does not take pleasure in afflicting even those that hate him, much less those that are walking in the ways of his commandments. He is not delighted with their pain and misery, but like a kind and loving Father, who considers the future well-being of his child, uses the rod only when nothing else will do. God does not always afflict on account of past sins or present follies, but often to turn us aside from evils to come. When he uses the rod, it is not for self-gratification, but to save those upon whom it falls. If Christians could only remember, while under chastisement, how kind and merciful their heavenly Father is, it would not only assist them to bear it, but even to kiss the rod, and draw nigh to him that handles it. But, alas! how frail and feeble we are; instead of being properly exercised thereby, we become fretful and disquieted, and can see nothing but clouds and darkness. "Afflictions are blessings to us, when we can bless God for them." "Whom the Lord loveth, he chasteneth, and scourgeth every son whom he receiveth." David, after having passed through some affliction, said it was good for him that he had been afflicted. So every Christian will feel in the end.

> "Aromatic plants bestow
> No spicy fragrance while they grow;
> But crushed or trodden to the ground,
> Diffuse their balmy sweets around."

Chastisements do not always come to us in the same dress. The wind may blow from any point of the compass. We can not tell to-day what its course will be to-morrow, nor whether it will be high or low. So afflictions and chastisements often visit us from quarters we had least expected, and at times we had not anticipated. The cup of pleasure already raised to our lips is often ruthlessly dashed away. But no matter in what garb afflictions come, they can not come without our Father's notice, yea, more, they can not come without his permission. Observation, history, and experience unite in witnessing that there is no pathway in life that is all the way smooth. There are rough places, rugged mountains, and broad rivers to cross; and it is best for us that it should be so. "Carefully refined food would be deleterious to the body; and God has mixed the coarse and fine in due proportions, so that together they nourish and expand the frame; and so carefully refined circumstances, spheres of action, would be deleterious to the soul; and God has mingled the rough and smooth; and he who takes them as God gives them, will be robust in his spiritual frame, and well developed in all the graces of the soul."

The benefits arising from chastisements and afflictions, when received in a proper spirit and with proper faith in God, are so manifold that only a few of them can be considered in this connection. The great purpose of God, as brought to light in his written word, is the salvation of as many as will come to him. And the means and instrumentalities employed to accomplish this grand result are as numerous as the stars of heaven. But all are under the direction of an all-wise, all-powerful, and ever-working Providence. All are intended to aid, in some way or other, in the ultimate salvation of those who are seeking to comply with the requirements of the gospel of his Son. He orders, permits, controls, and overrules surrounding circumstances so that each event, however insignificant it may appear, if properly received will aid in bringing his beloved to himself. And what now, in this time haze, seems to be against us will in the end be seen to have been all for the best. The saint at home, when the contest is over, will realize that that affliction, that sorrow, that bereavement, that disappointment, that loss, that turn, was just at the right time, and with the proper surroundings to save him from utter ruin.

> "If affliction grasps thee rudely,
> And presents the rack and cup,
> Drink the draught and brave the torture—
> Even in despair—look up!
> Still look up! For one there liveth
> With the will and power to save—
> One who knows each human sorrow,
> From the cradle to the grave."

One great benefit resulting from chastisement and affliction is that it reminds us of our weaknesses. We are ever prone to self-sufficiency.

The church at Laodicea had grown proud and haughty. They said they were rich and had need of nothing. Continued prosperity is almost sure to produce this kind of feeling. It is while under the influence of chastisement that Christians, as well as those that are not Christians, are brought to realize their own helplessness and want; it shows all how frail a thing humanity is. In this arrangement of divine providence there is such a manifestation of fatherly concern and love as is seldom if ever found in any other way. The church at Laodicea did not know how blind and miserable they were. Thus in long-continued prosperity men will forget God, and forget how exceedingly frail they are, and rush on to ruin. There is nothing that will produce in the soul a deeper sense of want than severe affliction. While under its influence, the world, with all its charms and allurements, will appear cold and cheerless. In prosperity the world appears to be full of charms, but while under the rod the charm is broken, the flowers wither and fall, while the Christian will look away to Jesus for comfort and strength. There is nothing in this wide world that can benefit a Christian more than that by or through which he is brought to realize that Christ is his only dependence. When Peter undertook to walk upon the water and began to sink,

he felt that there was but one chance for his life,—
"Lord Jesus, save me." It was well for Peter
that Jesus was there. God in his gracious providences often permits his disciples to have their
own way for a little while, that he may teach
them a lesson. Peter was bold and somewhat
rash. There was a great deal of human nature
about him, and Jesus permitted him to do what
he desired. It was a good lesson for Peter, and
no doubt humbled his pride. We must be taught
in the same school.

Paul said, "When I am weak, then am I strong."
In proportion as he was made to see and feel his
own weakness and insufficiency, he was able to lay
hold on Christ. God does not bestow spiritual
blessing upon the soul until it realizes its need of
them. "Blessed are they that do hunger and
thirst after righteousness, for they shall be filled."
Those that are thirsty are invited to come and
drink. Afflictions and chastisements are not sent
or permitted to visit us in order to destroy us, but
to instruct us. From them we can learn, more
readily than from prosperity, how weak and dependent we are. Christians while under the rod
should not allow themselves to believe that they
are forsaken. God is watching them all the time.
"There is an island in a distant sea, from whose
shores the fishermen sail in tiny crafts to procure

the treasures of the deep. During their absence thick mists often descend and cover highland, cliff, and beacon with so thick a veil that those hardy mariners are left without a mark by which to steer their laden bark. But in those dull hours they are not left to wander unguided on the pathless sea. When the time for their return arrives, the women of the islet—mothers, wives, sisters, and daughters,—descend to the shores and raise the voice of song. Borne on the quiet air, their voices soon fall sweetly on the ears of the loved ones on the sea. Guided by their well-known sounds, they steer their boats in safety to the shore. And thus to thee, O Christian, comes the voice of love from the celestial shore, as thou wanderest, a bewildered child of tribulation, on the misty sea of life. Hearken! 'Be of good cheer,' is the cry that greets thee. It comes from Jesus, who has overcome this world, which is the scene and source of your trials. His conquest over your adversary is the pledge of your victory, therefore 'be of good cheer.'"

> "How must yearn
> Our Lord's deep heart of love when saints are weeping!
> He whose creative breath first gave
> Flowers into earth, each tear will save,
> And smile it to a pearl in heaven's sure keeping."

Another source of consolation, under affliction

and chastisement, is that it serves as a means of trying our faith. "Examine yourselves, whether ye be in the faith." If our faith were never tried we should not know what its strength is. Bishop Hall says, "Untried faith is uncertain faith." It will be a serious, solemn matter to die— to pass from scenes familiar to those new and strange. Now if our faith was never tried until we reach the valley of the shadow of death, it might fail us at that critical moment. Any man may be deceived, for the heart of the natural man is deceitful above all things. "Be not deceived," is the solemn warning of the apostle. In the ordinary walks of life, when the sun is shining brightly, there is not much to test our faith. Peter said to the saints: "For a season, if need be, ye are in heaviness through manifold temptations: that the trial of your faith, being much more precious than of gold that perisheth, though it be tried with fire, might be found unto praise and and honor and glory at the appearing of Jesus Christ." I. Peter i. 6, 7. The plain, unambiguous meaning of the apostle is, that trials are sometimes necessary to try our faith. When we have no trials for a long time we grow careless. A good man said, "God can neither trust me with health nor money; therefore I am both poor and afflicted." We must be tried, else we should not know the character or strength of our faith. As gold is tried by fire, by which the dross and all the heterogeneous mixture are separated from it, so our faith is proved by afflictions and temptations. What is pure will stand the fire; and when the end is come the faith of the saints will shine like the purest gold, for it has been tried in the fire. "God himself will praise and honor such a faith, angels and men will honor it, and Christ will crown it with glory."

The faith of Abraham shone brightly as he stood on the summit of the mountain with his knife raised over the body of his obedient son. There before him lay the child of promise, in whose seed the nations of the earth were to be blessed. How this was to be accomplished he did not know, nor did he stop to inquire. That was God's business and not his. He went forward by faith; and never perhaps was the faith of any man more severely tried. There were two points especially that would try him: First, a faith that produced in him sufficient courage to go forward; and second, how God could make his promise good. But no matter how this might be brought about, he went forward. Never did the faith of any man shine more brightly than Abraham's did when he was descending from the mountain. He had gone through the furnace, and his faith came out shining like the purest gold; there was not one bit of dross left in it.

By afflictions, in one way and another, under the directing hand of a wise and merciful Providence, our faith is trained and strengthened. Richard Cecil went into his room one day and found his little daughter very cheerful and happy. A friend had given her a box containing some beautiful beads. She ran to him to exhibit her beautiful gift. Her father said, "Daughter, they are very beautiful; but now, my dear, throw them into the fire." This was an unexpected request, and of course a severe trial. "Now," said her father, "I shall not compel you to do it; I leave it to you; but you never knew papa ask you to do a thing that was not kind to you. I can not tell why, but if you can trust me do so." Here was a test, a real trial of faith. Then she reasoned on this wise: "I do not know why my father asks me to do this, but then he has always been kind to me, and I suppose it must be right, and will be for the best." Then summoning up all the courage and faith she had, she took the box with its precious contents, and did as her father asked her to do. The next day her father presented her with something she had long desired, and far more beautiful and valuable than what she had thrown into the fire. "Now," said her father, "my child,

I did this to teach you to trust in that good Father in heaven. Many a time in your life he will require you to give up and avoid what you can not see the reason for avoiding; but if you trust that Father as you have trusted me, you will always find it best."

> "If weak thy faith, why choose the harder side?
> We nothing know but what is marvelous;
> Yet what is marvelous we can't believe,
> So weak our reason, and so great our God;
> What most surprises in the sacred page,
> Or full as strange, or stranger, must be true,
> Faith is not reason's labor, but repose."

Another blessing coming from afflictions and chastisements is that it tends to detach the affections from earthly objects and raise them to heavenly objects. If men and women were in constant health and prosperity they would presently want to remain here forever. But when wave after wave passes over them,—now rich; now disappointed; now reduced to poverty; now suffering from the treachery of supposed friends; then, and with many not till then, will they begin to look for a better country; then their tried spirits will begin to sigh for a home far away, where trials will not reach them. Go into the hovel of the poor, where one trouble hath followed another in quick succession. Go into the chamber of Death, where the grim monster has just done his work, and some loved one lies cold and still in his arms; talk to the stricken ones about earthly comforts and amusements; tell them all about the glitter and show of this world, and they will tell you, perhaps, that its charms are all broken. To them this world looks like a dreary tomb, a vast howling wilderness. But if they are Christians they will tell you what they know about a better land, a home far away, where the storms and ills of life will never come. They will tell you also how they long to be away from life's sorrows and storms. But if they had not been smitten with a cold blast, they would have thought much better of this world and less of that world. An old philosopher said, "If my property had not perished, I should have perished." Another said, "No man is more unhappy than the man who is never in adversity. In other words, the greatest affliction in life is never to be afflicted." No man is so happy and safe as he who dwells most in thoughts of heaven; and there is nothing that will cause us to think more of heaven and heavenly things than severe afflictions and disappointments.

"Come then affliction, if my Father bids,
    And be my frowning friend; a friend that frowns
    Is better than a smiling enemy."

But lest some one might say that we attribute too much to afflictions, we will give a few passages from the Scriptures bearing directly upon this point. "Before I was afflicted I went astray: but now have I kept thy word. * * * It is good for me that I have been afflicted; that I might learn thy statutes." Ps. cxix. 67, 71. Punshon says, "Trial is God's glorious alchemistry, by by which the dross is left in the crucible. the baser metals are transmuted, and the character is riched with gold." But whatever may be the nature of our trouble,—whether it be afflictions, crosses, losses, or disappointments,—we should always remember that "whom the Lord loveth he chasteneth, and scourgeth every son whom he receiveth." And "if we be without chastisement, we are bastards and not sons." We should also remember that nothing can befall us without the permission of our heavenly Father. There is always some wise end to be accomplished by our chastisement. If Christians generally were as willing to submit to the order of Divine Providence as they are to find fault with his wisdom and goodness, they would be more benefited by his chastenings. "God is love," and "they that trust in him shall be as Mount Zion, which can not be moved."

"For as the mountains are round about Jerusalem, so the Lord is round about them that love him." "I will say of the Lord, He is my refuge and my fortress: my God; in him will I trust.

Surely he shall deliver thee from the snare of the fowler, and from the noisome pestilence. He shall cover thee with his feathers, and under his wings shalt thou trust."

"Yet, since the effects of providence, we find,
Are variously dispensed to human kind;
That vice triumphs and virtue suffers here,
A brand that sovereign justice can not bear;
Our reason prompts us to a future state,
The last appeal from fortune and from fate;
Where God's all-righteous ways will be declared;
The bad meet punishment, the good reward."

CHAPTER XIII.

THE NECESSITY, IMPORTANCE, AND ENCOURAGEMENTS TO SUBMIT TO THE PROVIDENCE OF GOD.

"Give me care,
By thankful patience, to prevent despair;
Fit me to bear whate'er thou shalt assign;
I kiss the rod, because the rod is thine."

If Christians were as diligent and earnest in cultivating their comforts as they are in cultivating their sorrows, they would see that they have but little to complain of. The Rev. E. Peabody, of America, some years ago, was compelled to resign his pastoral work on account of hemorrhage of the lungs. About the same time, his only child died and his wife lost the use of her eyes. His home was broken up, and his prospects for the future of this world were gloomy enough. One day he came into the room where his wife was, and she said to him, "I have been thinking of our situation here, and have determined to be submissive and patient." "Ah," said he, "that is a good resolution; let us see what we have to submit to. I will make a list of our trials. First, we have a home: we must submit to that; secondly, we have the comforts of life: we will submit to that; thirdly, we have each other; fourthly, we have a multitude of friends; fifthly, we have God to take care of us." "Ah," said his wife, "I pray you to stop and I will say no more about submission." Thus let Christians, when they feel a disposition to murmur or complain, sit down and write out a list of their blessings and comforts, and then compare it with a list of their trials, which most persons keep constantly on hand, and it will be seen that the list of comforts and blessings is much longer than the list of trials. Dr. Hay, an eminent English surgeon, when injured apparently for life, said, "If it be the will of God that I should be confined to my sofa, and he command me to pick straws during the remainder of my life, I hope I shall feel no repugnance to his good pleasure."

It is a fatal error with many Christians, that they have fallen into the habit of looking on the dark side of almost everything. Whenever they are compelled to walk in a shadow, they at once conclude that it must be dark everywhere; forgetting that it requires light to make a shadow. There must be light somewhere, else there could be no such thing as a shadow. Moreover, God is as surely present in the shadow as in the sunbeam.

Dr. Beaumont reckons the following as among

the advantages arising from entire submission to the operations of divine providence. 1. "It will prevent rash conclusions—such as Jacob's in regard to Joseph, when he said, 'All these things are against me.' 2. It will prevent immoderate sorrow. 3. It will prevent sinful staggerings. Abraham staggered not. 4. It will give to us inward peace. 5. It will produce enduring happiness. 6. It will excite praise and thanksgiving." If you would find a happy man, go to one who is in complete harmony with the providences of God. No matter whether he is rich or poor, sick or well, he is happy with the blessed consciousness that God is doing all things well. "Patience is a plaster for all sores. The longest day will have an end. When one door shuts another opens." "All comes right to him who can wait."

Want of harmony with the providences of God has robbed the best of Christians of more solid, lasting consolation than any one thing. Dissatisfaction with the doings of the Almighty,—calling in question his wisdom, goodness, and mercy,—arraigning him before a human tribunal, and questioning his right to reign and rule, and then denouncing such part of his administration as is not in accordance with our notions—is a grievous insult to the goodness, love, and benevolence of the all-wise Creator. Oh, yes, when the sun shines brightly, and all nature smiles sweetly, and prosperity in her robe of white greets us at every nook and corner, it is easy enough to look up to heaven and say: "Father, thou hast done all things well." Even an infidel, under similar circumstances, could say as much. But when thick, dark clouds gather about us, and hoarse thunders crash over our heads; when adversity, like some heinous ghost, stares at us from every corner, and we are driven to the wall, then it requires something above nature to enable us to look up and say: "Father, it is well." Blessed be God, there is that in "pure religion" which will enable its possessor at all times, and in all places, to acquiesce in the workings of divine providence.

In order to submit to the operations of divine providence, we must, in the first place, have clear and correct views of God's sovereignty. Whatever we have belongs to him. The earth with its fullness; and the heavens with all its starry host is his also. We must realize that it is his right to withhold as he pleases. Riches and poverty, sickness and health, life and death, prosperity and adversity, are all at his disposal. We must feel that it is his right to rule, for "he doeth according to his will in the army of heaven, and among the inhabitants of the earth." Dan. iv. 35. There must also be proper conceptions of the righteousness and justice of the government of God. Whilst it is his right to do all things according to the counsel of his own will, he does it in perfect harmony with the principles of a righteous, moral government. Mysterious and inexplicable as his operations may sometimes appear to us, we must feel that he is doing right, that he is just and righteous altogether. The mercy, goodness, long-suffering, benevolence, and love of God is, or should be, a sufficient guaranty to every Christian, that whatever he does is necessary and right. God is perfect, ever full, and overflowing with blessings. If in his wisdom he sees it is best to take away what we have, he is abundantly able to give a hundred-fold in its place. He permitted Job to be stripped of all he had, and then gave him twice as much in its place. Heine, of Berlin, lost very heavily. Hufeland met him soon after, and expressed his sympathy. "I had rather you had not reminded me of it," he replied. "Thank God! I have got over it." "How have you managed that?" "Well, I was unable to forget it: thought upon it night and day; my mind was wandering, my family were sad and timid with fear. I felt that this must not continue; so I, a poor worm of the dust, unable to come out of this distress, took refuge in the Almighty. I hurried to my bed-room, closed the door behind me, and fell on my knees to pray with my whole heart. Then I felt as if God appeared to me saying, 'Have I not the key of all treasures? and can I not far more than replace the loss? Be of good courage.' And now I have got over it, and am once more happy in God." The greatest gain sometimes comes from the heaviest losses.

The prodigal son thought of home, but not until he had lost all, and was pressed with want. But for this, he would have continued a prodigal. When Job's things were taken away, he thought more of God and knew more about him than he had ever known before. So while God in the wisdom and goodness of his providence takes away in one thing, he will more than restore in something else. God will not allow himself to be in debt to any member of his family. If he causes or permits his beloved to be cast into the furnace, it is only that he may be purified. If there were no dross about him, he would never see the furnace. "Fire and hammer and file are necessary to give the metal form; and it must have many a grind and many a rub ere it will shine; so in trial, character is shaped and beautified and brightened."

> "A bruised reed he will not break—
> Affliction all his children feel;
> He wounds them for his mercy's sake—
> He wounds to heal."

No man, however wise he may be, can know in advance what is best for him. All desire to be saved, and sometimes express a willingness to submit to almost anything if that end may be reached, yet when brought to the test are unwilling to yield cheerful obedience to the will of God. Can any man reasonably suppose that a God of power, wisdom, and goodness, would do anything wrong, or suffer anything to befall his children that was not best for them? Unthinking people would have a world where everything grew spontaneously. They would not have a trial, nor a sorrow, nor a care, nor a pain, nor a disappointment. They would be fanned by breezes balmier than those that blew over Eden in the early morning of time. They would have everything that heart could wish. They would have summer but no winter, roses but no thorns, joy but no sorrow, life but no death. Now Faith says, If these things were best for us, our heavenly Father would straightway give them to us; but seeing they are denied us, it is sufficient evidence that we will be better off in the end without them. What a beauty there is in entire submission to the will of God, by means of which we cheerfully surrender all things,—life, friends, time, and eternity into his hands. Mr. John Bates gives an incident by which this is beautifully illustrated. "A brother and sister were once playing in a field, when he lost a ring, which was the Christmas gift of a friend, his choicest earthly treasure. After searching for it in vain, he went with many tears to a retired spot, kneeled, and prayed most earnestly. And did God answer his prayer, so that he found the ring? No. But, said the little boy, he made me happy to lose it. Christian mother, have you lost your only earthly treasure, and have you gone to the throne of grace in prayer, and found that though you could not find again your much-loved child, God has made you happy to lose it? Have you, bereaved wife, husband, sister, brother, friend? Oh, when we can feel happy to lose *any* blessing which our heavenly Father hath given us and then taken away we are beautifully resigned to his will." A Christian lady was ill, and being asked whether she desired to live or die, replied: "Which God pleaseth." "But," one said, "if God were to refer it to you, which would you choose?" "Truly," she said, "if God were to refer it to me I would even refer it to him again." No soul on earth drinks so deeply from the fountain of happiness as that one which has surrendered all to God.

"To do, or not to do; to have,
Or not to have; I leave to thee:
To be, or not to be, I leave;
Thy only will be done in me!
All my requests are lost in one—
'Father, thy will be done!'

> Welcome alike the crown or cross;
> Trouble I can not ask, nor peace;
> Nor toil, nor rest, nor gain, nor loss;
> Nor joy, nor grief, nor pain, nor ease;
> Nor life, nor death;—but ever groan,
> 'Father, thy will be done.'"

As a ground of encouragement to submit to all the workings of providence, God has given unto us exceeding great and precious promises. They are to the believer an inexhaustible mine of wealth—an armory filled with weapons, offensive and defensive. They are as high as heaven, deep as the grave, and vast as the universe. No one can tell how precious the promises are, until he has leaned his whole weight upon them. "No valley of trouble will be to him without a door of hope; no barren wilderness without manna; no dry rock without water; no dungeon without light; no fiery trial without comfort, because he hath the same word and the same God to trust to, whose power opened the sea as a door, to be a passage from Egypt to Canaan; who fed Israel in the wilderness with bread from heaven, and water from the rock; who filled Peter's prison with a shining light; who made the three children to walk to and fro amidst the fiery furnace with joy and gladness." Christian, can you not afford to trust in such a God?

A pious old slave, on a Virginia plantation, was

asked why he was always so happy and contented with his hard lot? "Ah! massa, I always lays flat down on de promises, and den I prays straight up to my hebenly Father." The promises of God are the Christian's Magna Charta; they are heaven's own bonds, issued by the authority of him whose name is Jehovah. Heaven and earth may pass away, but every promise, to the last word, will be fulfilled. God is immutable and can not lie; he is abundantly able to do all he has promised. The whole Trinity is pledged to fulfill every word that hath been spoken. "No music is half so sweet, no eloquence is near so charming, no picture is at all so attractive, as the precious promises given to us by the faithful and true Witness. Like the aurora borealis shining on the frosty, somber sky, tinging it with beautiful colors and relieving it with brilliant rays, the promises of the gospel shine in tints of light and smiles of love on the cold and gloomy night of trouble, cheering the heart of every child of God with delightful tokens of the presence and the kindness of his heavenly Father."

There is no pathway in life exempt from trials and afflictions; no day without its night; no rose without its thorn; no valley without its hills and mountains. But, as an off-set to all this, there is a promise to meet every possible case. Jesus has gone over the whole length of the way, not by proxy, but in person. He has drank at every fountain, passed through every valley, ascended every rugged mountain, passed over every desert, crossed every stream, and has thoroughly prepared the way. And there is not a passable inch of the way but is well covered with the most precious promises. And the beauty of this wise arrangement of providence is, that when you come to a mountain, or river, or desert, you are not to wait until the promise is given; it is there before you. Whoever will submit all into the hands of God, will find in the end that all things were made subservient in some way or other to their highest good.

> "Abroad, at home, in weal, in woe,
> That service which to heaven you owe,
> That bounden service duly pay,
> And God shall be your strength alway."

It will not be possible to enumerate all the promises in this connection. A few of the many must suffice. And while your attention may be directed to some of the precious promises of the gospel, I would desire also to fix your attention on the power, wisdom, immutability, and benevolence of God. Every promise is secured to us by all that is in heaven and in the earth. They will and must be fulfilled just at the right time and in the right place. The Lord said to Jacob, and through him to all that would believe: "Behold, I am with thee, and will keep thee in all places whither thou goest, and will bring thee again into this land; for I will not leave thee, until I have done that which I have spoken to thee of." Gen. xxviii. 15. What God promised to the Old Testament saints, is applicable to the saints of all ages. These promises are all leaves from the same tree of life. In this promise the saints have the assurance that God will be present at all times. When he said to Jacob I will not leave thee, but be with thee, he meant more than that universal presence which is alike everywhere. He meant that he would be present to direct, counsel, protect, help, sustain, and defend him. In like manner God has been with his people in all time past. Thus he was with the Hebrews in the furnace; with Daniel in the lion's den; with the apostles in prison. In this promise he not only offers his gifts, but himself: "I will go with thee." Resting on the veracity of God, Abraham, when called immediately obeyed and went out, not knowing where he went. It was not necessary that he should know whither he went, since God had promised to go with him. Now, Christian, what about the future? Does it look dark and gloomy? Are you afraid of trials and difficulties? Hear what your Father has said: "Fear thou not; for I am with thee: be not dismayed; for I am thy God: I will strengthen thee; yea, I will uphold thee with the right hand of my righteousness." Isa. xli. 10. Could you ask more than this? Whatever there is in God, of help, strength, power, wisdom, goodness, love, and comfort, is herein and hereby made over to the believer. What road is too rough to travel, since God has said, "I am with thee?" What cross is too heavy to bear, since God has said, "I will strengthen thee?" What burden is too heavy to bear, since God has said, "I will uphold thee?" What is too hard to do, since God has said, "Yea, I will help thee."

The safety of the believer, under the most trying circumstances in which he may by the providence of God be placed, is most graciously, and I may say gloriously, provided for. "Lord, increase our faith." For if we have faith like a grain of mustard seed, we will realize a perfect security under all circumstances. Listen to the voice of God: "When thou passest through the waters, I will be with thee; and through the rivers, they shall not overflow thee: when thou walkest through the fire, thou shalt not be burned; neither shall the flame kindle upon thee." Isa. xliii. 2. "The Lord is on my side; I will not fear:

what can man do unto me?" Ps. cxviii. 6. Can you think of anything more? Is there anything that you will be likely to need, that is not included in these promises? Can you not well afford to trust everything to the wisdom, power, goodness, and veracity of such a Father! After having made such promises, would he lead or suffer you to be led into difficulties from which he could not or would not deliver you? Has he not said plainly, positively, that he would go with you, and help you? Mark the nature of the promises. He has not said that you shall not have afflictions, trials, and tribulations. He has said the very reverse: "In the world ye shall have tribulation;" "yea, all that live godly in Christ Jesus shall suffer persecution." These things are plainly taught, and the believer may look for them. But God has said: "I will be with thee;" "I will help thee;" "I will uphold thee;" "I will lead thee;" "I will strengthen thee;" "I will guide thee;" "I will never leave thee, nor forsake thee." Christian, will that do? Can you think of anything more? If you can, it must be included in that other promise which says. "No good thing will he withhold from them that walk uprightly;" or in this one, "For all things are yours; whether Paul, or Apollos, or Cephas. or the world, or life, or death, or things present, or things to come; all are yours; and ye are Christ's; and Christ is God's." I. Cor. iii. 21–23.

"But," says the timid one,—and there are many such,—"the future still looks dark and foreboding. I fear the afflictions and tribulations which will surely come upon me." Allow me to direct you to some promises relating to those under afflictions and trials. "I know that the Lord will maintain the cause of the afflicted, and the right of the poor." Ps. cxl. 12. "Blessed be God, even the Father of our Lord Jesus Christ, the Father of mercies, and the God of all comfort; who comforteth us in all our tribulation, that we may be able to comfort them which are in any trouble, by the comfort wherewith we ourselves are comforted of God." II. Cor. i. 3, 4. "He shall call upon me, and I will answer him: I will be with him in trouble; I will deliver him, and honor him." Ps. xci. 15. The sure promise of God is that the believer shall be supported and upheld in all his afflictions. No matter how severe they may be, God will maintain his cause. God has not only promised to support and uphold in affliction, but will at the proper time deliver from it. "Many are the afflictions of the righteous: but the Lord delivereth him out of them all. He keepeth all his bones: not one of them is broken." Ps. xxxiv. 19–20. "Thou hast turned for me my mourning into dancing: thou hast put off my sackcloth, and girded me with gladness." Ps. xxx. 11.

There are numerous figures used by the sacred writers to teach us that whatever may be the afflictions, temptations, and trials of the righteous, they are of but short duration,—"for a season," "a day of adversity," "the hour of temptation," "light affliction, which is but for a moment." You will not be left in the crucible a moment longer than will be necessary to separate the dross from the gold. A few ladies were in the habit of meeting at each others' houses for the purpose of studying the Scriptures. When they came to the third chapter of Malachi, the conversation turned on the method of purifying silver. They desired to know what was meant by the language, "He shall sit as a refiner, and purifier of silver." So one of the ladies visited a silversmith and inquired of him: "Do you sit during the operation of purifying?" "Yes," was the reply, "for I must keep my eye steadily on the furnace, lest the silver become injured by the intense heat." "But how do you know when it is pure?" "When I can see my own face reflected in the metal." Are you in the furnace of affliction? Jesus is sitting close by: his eye is upon you, and when he can see his own image reflected in you the heat will be removed.

"He that from dross would win the precious ore,
Bends o'er the crucible an earnest eye,
The subtle searching process to explore,
Lest the one brilliant moment should pass by
When in the molten silver's virgin mass
He meets his pictured face as in a glass.
Thus in God's furnace are his people tried;
Thrice happy they who to the end endure.
But who the fiery trial may abide?
Who from the crucible come forth so pure
That he whose eyes of flame look through the whole
May see his image perfect in the soul?'

The apostle, before whose eye this world did not present a very flattering prospect, felt that whatever there was of the world was entirely safe in the hands of God. "Casting all your care upon him; for he careth for you." I. Pet. v. 7. "Whatever things concern a follower of God, whether in themselves great or small, God concerns himself with them; what affects them affects him; in all their afflictions he is afflicted. He who knows that God cares for him, need have no anxious cares about himself. He will bear both thee and thy burden." Paul says: "I know whom I have believed, and am persuaded that he is able to keep that which I have committed to him against that day." The apostle had made an entire consecration of himself to Christ, and had the utmost confidence in his ability and willingness to keep all he had committed to him. If you have made a full and complete consecration of all you have and are to God, then you have nothing to dread. Let trials come if they must; let the lion roar if he will; let the hurricane blow if it choose—trust in God and go forward singing, "The Lord is my shepherd; I shall not want. He maketh me to lie down in green pastures: he leadeth me beside the still waters. Yea, though I walk through the valley of the shadow of death, I will fear no evil: for thou art with me; thy rod and thy staff they comfort me." Your enemy may whisper in your ear as he did in the psalmist's, that "there is no help for him in God." But that is not true—not one word of truth in it. And the devil himself knows that it is false; for God has said to his beloved, "I will never leave thee, nor forsake thee." "It is I, be not afraid."

Peter took a most cheerful view of the trials, temptations, and conflicts of a Christian's life. "Beloved, think it not strange concerning the fiery trial which is to try you, as though some strange thing happened unto you: but rejoice, inasmuch as ye are partakers of Christ's sufferings; that, when his glory shall be revealed, ye may be glad also with exceeding joy. If ye be reproached for the name of Christ, happy are ye; for the Spirit of glory and of God resteth upon you." I. Pet. iv. 12–14. It is no strange thing for Christians to be persecuted, tempted, and tried: it was so from the beginning; but to suffer for Christ's sake and in Christ's cause was always honorable. Besides, the sufferer has the blessed assurance that he shall be sustained and upheld in life, and afterward received up into glory. Fiery trials are not intended to destroy, only to try the children of God. One of two things is secured by promise: the burden will be lifted from the shoulder of the believer, or he will receive strength to bear it. When the Almighty Savior sees that it is not best to lighten the load, he will help him to carry it. Paul had a heavy load laid on him, and he asked that it might be lifted. But for wise and good reasons the burden was not removed. But the Lord did what was just as good, and perhaps better, for he said to him, "My grace is sufficient." Come what will, the mercy of the Lord endureth forever. "The mountains shall depart, and the hills be removed; but my kindness shall not depart from thee, neither shall the covenant of my peace be removed, saith the Lord that hath mercy on thee." St. Augustine said: "Behold us willing to suffer in this life the most it may please thee to bring upon us; here lay thy rod upon us; 'consume us here, cut us to pieces here, only spare us in eternity.'" Jeremiah said (Jer. x. 24), "O **Lord**, correct me, but with judgment; not in thine anger, lest thou bring me to nothing."

Mr. Rutherford, in conversation with a lady who had spoken complainingly of her trials, said: "Madam, when ye are come to the other side of the water, and have set down your foot on the shore of glorious eternity, and look again to the waters and to your wearisome journey, and shall see, in that clear glass of endless glory, nearer to the bottom of God's wisdom, ye shall then be forced to say, 'If God had done otherwise with me than he hath done, I had never come to the enjoyment of this crown of glory.'" Christian,

> "Stand but your ground, your ghastly foes will fly—
> He trembles at a heaven-directed eye;
> Choose rather to defend than to assail—
> Self-confidence will in the conflict fail:
> When you are challenged, you may dangers meet—
> True courage is a fixed, not sudden heat;
> Is always humble, lives in self-distrust,
> And will itself into no danger thrust.
> Devote yourself to God, and you will find
> God fights the battles of a will resigned
> Love Jesus! Love will no base fear endure—
> Love Jesus! And of conquest rest secure."

I know of no way by which a Christian can escape temptation. Satan will often assault the the soul; but no matter, this should not frighten the believer. The apostle said to the church at that day, and to us as well, that "there hath no temptation taken you but such as is common to man: but God is faithful, who will not suffer you to be tempted above that ye are able; but will with the temptation also make a way to escape, that ye may be able to bear it." All the powers of earth and hell combined can never close in on all sides of a Christian. God will see to it that a door is kept open—a way to escape. God has said it, and so it shall be. The contest with Satan would indeed be fatal to every Christian if God were not present to defend and help. But he is always near, and always ready to sustain.

Bring together all your trials, conflicts, pain, poverty, weakness, temptations, chastisements, sorrows, losses, disappointments, and persecutions; then add all the trials, including death itself, that you ever expect to have, and lay them all down together; then turn to the precious promises of the gospel, and see if there is not enough to cover them over as many times as there are stars in the heavens. See if there is any possible case that is not most gloriously provided for in the gracious promises of the gospel. God foresaw all the conflicts his children would have, and made the most ample provision for them. "For in the time of trouble he shall hide me in his pavilion: in the secret of his tabernacle shall he hide me; he shall set me up upon a rock." Ps. xxvii. 5. "The righteous cry, and the Lord heareth, and delivereth them out of all their troubles." Ps. xxxiv.17. "But thou hast fully known my doctrine, manner of life, purpose, faith, long-suffering, charity, patience, persecutions, afflictions, which came unto me at Antioch, at Iconium, at Lystra; what persecutions I endured: but out of them all the Lord delivered me." II. Tim. iii, 10–11. "No weapon that is formed against thee shall prosper; and every tongue that shall rise against thee in judgment thou shalt condemn. This is the heritage of the servants of the Lord, and their righteousness is of me, saith the Lord." Isaiah liv. 17. "But the Lord is with me as a mighty terrible one: therefore my persecutors shall stumble, and they shall not prevail: they shall be greatly ashamed; for they shall not prosper: their everlasting confusion shall never be forgotten." Jer. xx. 11.

Add to the promises already enumerated those that relate more directly to the future, and you will have a fortification which will stand, though the heavens fall. "Ye shall have a crown of life." "A house not made with hands." "Many mansions." "An inheritance, incorruptible, undefiled, and that fadeth not away." "Eternal life." "A city which hath foundations." Then take the negatives. "No sickness." "No pain." "No sorrow, nor sighing." "No death." "No sin." "And there shall be no night there."

With such promises as these to lean on, one would suppose that a Christian could endure any storm, and bear up in any conflict; more especially when we remember that whatever afflictions, chastisements, and trials a Christian has, which are not removed, are intended, under the control and management of a wise and gracious providence, to assist in some way in preparing the soul for higher and purer joys. Spencer, when speaking of the benefits of trials, says: "Stars shine brightest in the darkest night; torches are the better for beating; grapes come not to the proof till they come to the press; spices smell sweetest when pounded; young trees root the faster for shaking; vines are the better for bleeding; gold looks the brighter for scouring; glowworms glisten best in the dark; juniper smells sweetest in the fire; powder becomes most fragrant for chasing; the palm-tree proves the better for pressing; camomile, the more you tread it the more you spread it. Such is the condition of all God's children; they are the most triumphant when most tempted; most in the favor of God when least in man's; as their conflicts, so their conquests; as their tribulation, so their triumphs."

Entire submission to the will of God, in all the operations of divine Providence, is the highest and most glorious state to which a saint, while on earth, can attain. In this state, the soul is brought into such spiritual union and communion with Jesus Christ, that whatever may occur, it will be right. "To live is Christ, to die is gain." In this state the soul has no choice, only to do the will of God. When Ex-Governor Wright, of Indiana, was near the close of his life, his wife, while conducting the morning devotions, prayed most devoutly that God would bless the means being used for the recovery of her husband. Mr. Wright stopped her in the midst of her prayer and said, "My dear, I would rather hear you pray, 'Thy will, O God, be done.'" In a few hours afterward, he calmly fell asleep in Jesus. Harmony with the providences of God will bring peace and consolation to the heart, no matter how severely the storms rage without. Christians should always remember that they can suffer the will of God, as well as do the will of God. When the tyrant threatened Socrates with death, the old philosopher, stoic-like, said he was willing to die. "Nay, then," said the tyrant, "you shall live against your will." "Nay, but," said Socrates, "whatever you do with me, it shall be my will." Now, if a pagan philosopher, who was not at all certain about the future existence of man, could so surrender himself to the will of a tyrant, what doth hinder a Christian from surrendering his all into the hands of God, and submitting to his will? especially when he has the most positive assurance that he will be sustained in all his tribulations, and in the end received up into glory.

The prospect of future blessedness should encourage the believer to submit most cheerfully to the providences of God. Weeping may endure for a night, but joy cometh in the morning. He may suffer to-day and to-morrow, and the next day be with the angels. Who, when the conflict is over, will repine or complain of the trials he has had? Who will then find fault with the chastenings of the Lord? Who will care for the rugged mountains he has climbed, or the dark valleys he has gone through? The conflict is over and past, and

"The soul for joy will fold her wings,
And loud her lovely sonnet sing,
I am safe at home."

The bright visions of the better land, to the dying saint, cause him to forget the conflicts of the past. When Moses had reached the summit of the mountain, and gained a glimpse of the promised land, he seemed not to notice the valley and the river that lay between' him and the land of milk and honey. So the weary, tired Christian, as he nears his heavenly home, will lose sight of the past, and overlook the valley and river of death, and long to be gone. God has as well provided for the death of his beloved as for his life. Christians die in a state of gracious security. The time, place, and circumstances are all foreseen and provided for.

A few incidents illustrating God's provisions for his children in their conflict with the last enemy, may not be improper in this connection. They may serve to comfort and cheer those that are timid. God will not only sustain his children while living, but also when dying. They will live long enough, and die soon enough. They will die in the right place, with the right disease, and under the right circumstances. Senator Foot, of Vermont, when dying, said: "I have been thinking much of these two lines:

> 'Here, Lord, I give myself away;
> 'Tis all that I can do!'

I begin to understand that this comprehends all; and I am beginning to lean alone on Jesus Christ as my only Savior and Friend. I see it, I see it; the gates are wide open! Beautiful; beautiful!" and immediately expired.

Robert Bruce, a Scotch minister, while sitting at the breakfast table, requested his daughter to bring him some article of food. She started to comply with his request, when he said, "Hold, daughter, hold! my Master calleth me." Here his sight failed; but he called for a Bible and requested his daughter to place his fingers on the passage, "I am persuaded that neither life no death shall be able to separate me from the love of God, which is in Christ Jesus my Lord." He then said: "God be with you, my children. I have breakfasted with you, and shall sup with my Lord Jesus Christ this night." These were his last words.

An aged Christian lady, living in a poor-house, but well resigned to the will of God, was one day conversing with a minister, and gave evidence of great inward peace. When asked why she seemed to feel so inexpressibly happy, she replied, "O sir, I was just thinking what a change it will be from the poor-house to heaven."

A dying father said to his family that he wanted to talk with them about heaven. This alarmed his daughter, who had not till then thought her father to be so near death. "Surely," said she, "you do not think there is any danger?" Calmly he replied: "Daughter, my darling! Oh! do not use that word. There can be no danger to the Christian, whatever may happen. All is right; all is well. God is love. All is well—

everlastingly well!" Thus a Christian, who is fully resigned to the will of God, and in perfect harmony with all his providences, will feel, whether living or dying.

Bunyan said: "Let dissolution come when it will, it can do the Christian no harm; for it will be but a passage out of a prison into a palace; out of a sea of trouble into a haven of rest; out of a crowd of enemies to an innumerable company of true, loving, and faithful friends; out of shame, reproach, and contempt, into exceeding great and eternal glory." J. Harvey said: "Oh, welcome, Death! thou mayest well be reckoned among the treasures of the Christian. The great conflict is over; all is done. To live is Christ; but to die is gain." Dr. Preston said: "Blessed be God; though I change my place, I shall not change my company; for I have walked with God while living, and now I go to rest with God." J. Parson said: "When I get to glory I will make heaven ring with my voice, and wave my palm over the heads of the saints, crying, "Victory, victory, in the blood of the Lamb!" Alexander Mather said: "He whom I have served for near fifty years will not forsake me now. Glory be to God and the Lamb forever and ever."

Weary, tired one, be of good cheer; you s all rest by and by. Cast all your cares and sorrows upon him who has said, "I will never leave thee nor forsake thee." Then, when you have served and suffered the will of God you will be received to your home of many mansions. Then you will see, in a clearer, brighter light, that God hath done all things well. Saved! Victory through the blood of the Lamb. At home. Rest! "And there shall be no night there."

"No night shall be in heaven; no gathering gloom
Shall over that glorious landscape ever come;
No tears shall fall in sadness over those flowers
That breathe their fragrance through celestial bowers.

"No night shall be in heaven; no darkened room,
No bed of death, nor silence of the tomb;
But breezes ever fresh with love and truth
Shall brace the frame with an immortal youth.

"No night shall be in heaven, oh, had I faith
To rest in what the faithful witness saith,
That faith should make these hideous phantoms flee
And leave no night henceforth on earth to me."

www.ingramcontent.com/pod-product-compliance
Lightning Source LLC
Chambersburg PA
CBHW030745230426

43667CB00007B/851